Samuel A. Swiggett

Bright Side of Prison Life

Experiences, in prison and out, of an involuntary sojourner in rebeldom

Samuel A. Swiggett

Bright Side of Prison Life
Experiences, in prison and out, of an involuntary sojourner in rebeldom

ISBN/EAN: 9783744758741

Printed in Europe, USA, Canada, Australia, Japan

Cover: Foto ©ninafisch / pixelio.de

More available books at **www.hansebooks.com**

CAPT. S. A. SWIGGETT.

THE
Bright Side of Prison Life.

Experiences, In Prison and Out, of an Involuntary Sojourner in Rebeldom.

By CAPTAIN S. A. SWIGGETT.

PRICE $1.25.

Press of
FLEET, McGINLEY & CO.
Baltimore

PREFACE.

The author's name and reputation may sell this book—miracles have happened; but he does not intend to permit the possible deception of a confiding public into the belief that they cannot exist without reading it. The possible purchaser is hereby warned that it is different from any other book he ever read. It is without plot, moral, historical value, mystery, romance, horrors and murderous scenes. The best excuse to be offered for its existence is the fact that the author's numerous friends have repeatedly urged him to print what they call an interesting and unusual series of incidents. The responsibility for any injury to the public must rest upon the heads of these friends, the author not holding himself accountable for anything except the truth of the narration. My friends being pleased with this publication, it may be safe for others to try it, but they must not blame me for any lack of appreciation. Trusting that this warning will prevent the unsuspecting from buying the book solely on account of the author's literary reputation, the result is awaited with fear and trembling.

S. A. SWIGGETT.

March, 1895.

CONTENTS.

CHAPTER I.
                                                                     Page
Preliminaries 9

CHAPTER II.
The Capture.................................. 18

CHAPTER III.
On the March.................................. 27

CHAPTER IV.
Bright Spots.................................. 39

CHAPTER V.
The Stockade.................................. 44

CHAPTER VI.
Incidents 53

CHAPTER VII.
Events 61

CHAPTER VIII.
An Escape.................................. 69

CHAPTER IX.
On the Tramp.................................. 77

CHAPTER X.
Recaptured 85

CHAPTER XI.
The Back Track.................................. 93

CHAPTER XII.
The Return to the Stockade.............................. 103

CHAPTER XIII.
Incidents, and Another Escape........................... 109

CHAPTER XIV.
Tramps Once More....................................... 120

CHAPTER XV.
Diplomacy 129

CHAPTER XVI.
Making Progress.. 139

CHAPTER XVII.
A Puzzle, and Incidents................................ 148

CHAPTER XVIII.
Experiences 158

CHAPTER XIX.
Good Luck and Bad...................................... 169

CHAPTER XX.
In the Toils... 177

CHAPTER XXI.
Another Return Trip.................................... 186

CHAPTER XXII.
Foraging, and a New Prison............................. 196

CHAPTER XXIII.
To Camp Ford and Joy................................... 207

CHAPTER XXIV.
Liberty at Last.. 219

ILLUSTRATIONS.

Captain S. A. Swiggett,	Frontispiece.
General F. M. Drake,	18
Lieutenant Walter S. Johnson,	39
Adjutant S. K. Mahon,	69
Captain J. B. Gedney,	79
Captain Thomas M. Fee,	89
Captain Charles Burnbaum,	94
Captain J. P. Rummel,	115
Captain B. F. Miller,	167
Sergeant E. B. Rocket,	189

The Bright Side of Prison Life.

CHAPTER I.

PRELIMINARIES.

My first appearance in the United States was made on the 19th of May, A. D. 1834. I have no recollection of this important event, but am reliably informed that the given date is correct, and that Dorchester county, Maryland, was the locality. At that time I had no premonition of my future life in a rebel prison, and if anyone had told me of the fourteen months which were to be spent mostly in such a manner I should have paid no attention whatever.

The year 1855 found me in Blakesburg, Iowa, after having lived in Indiana during the three years following my removal from Maryland.

In 1856 occurred my marriage to Miss Eliza H. Van Cleve, and no man could be more happily wedded. For thirty-eight years, until her recent death, on April 13, 1894, our life was as much of a honeymoon as it is possible for a well-mated couple to make it.

I had learned the trade of a tailor, but other employment offered more inducements, and, on

August 8, 1862, my occupation was that of postmaster at Blakesburg, Iowa, keeping a small general store in connection with the postoffice. On this date I enlisted with others, and we were sworn in at our place.

Our company was organized at Ottumwa, where we went for the purpose, and my election as first lieutenant gave me much pleasure. Here we spent about two weeks at squad drill, having the usual experience of beginners.

Many of the town girls had lovers, brothers and relatives in our company, and we had many fair critics present at our drills on the south bank of the Des Moines river. The excitement was great at the time, and everybody seemed to be interested very much in our company. For a while we received the criticisms of our fair guests with equanimity, but at last we conceived the idea of turning the tables, and soon had an opposition company so interested in their own drill that the girls gave us some peace. Two of the boys afterwards married members of the competing company.

We rendezvoused at Keokuk, where the 36th Iowa Infantry was finally organized and mustered into the service of the United States on October 4, 1862, Col. Charles W. Kitredge commanding. Our boys were designated Company B.

About November 1 the regiment went to Benton Barracks, near St. Louis, and remained until December 20. After we were ordered to go south all was bustle till we embarked on two steamboats and started on our voyage.

The boats were loaded to the guards with soldiers, hard tack and coffins, the last being piled up in all available space. Said Pat Riley, a member of our company: "Holy Jasus, byes, luk! Luk at that! Hev us ter kerry thim ter hev 'em handy loike?"

The mute suggestion of the many coffins was not pleasant, but our boys were hopeful, and many jokes were bandied about in consequence of their presence.

That sail down the mighty river will never be forgotten. None knew where we were going, and the conflict between hope and fear was in many a breast—hope of success and glory, and distrust of the issue. On board all was confusion; oaths, laughter, witty remarks, hoarse orders, din in general. Looking inboard, one could forget all save the immediate present, and hope was predominant. Looking up at the sky, with its sweeping clouds, like vast billows of dark, stormy sea, rushing on and tumbling over each other in mad haste, one felt the immensity of the universe and the littleness of man, despite his thunders of war. Listening to the asthmatic breathing of the "scape" pipes, and watching the shores gliding by, one half fancied a flight in the grasp of some huge monster that was bearing away its prey. Looking over the side and hearing the sob and swash of the seething water under the guards, one could imagine a restraining hand on the huge mass, the panting breath of exertion, and a moan of regret because of ineffectual effort to keep back the floating giant that was carrying so many human beings away to death and disaster. Fear of the future now became the paramount feeling.

We were halted at Memphis by a signal from shore, and found that the citizens and military authorities were in fear of an attack by Forrest. That night we slept on our arms in Jackson Square.

The next day some mule sheds were emptied of their living contents, and our boys were quartered in the vacated premises. We were then detailed for guard duty at Fort Pickering, which service we performed for several days, still having the privilege of enjoying our commodious quarters. It was hardly fair to turn the mules out into the cold to give shelter to a regiment of new recruits, but as the mules made no "kick" at this change, why should we object?

The spare hours of my first night as officer of the guard were spent in trying to get some sleep on the ground. It was raining hard, and it seemed impossible to find any spots which were not hollows; at any rate, I could not lie down without finding myself in a pool of water when

I awoke. My reflections and comments need not be recorded.

Christmas passed with scarcely a knowledge of the fact, and about the first of the year we were sent to Helena, Ark., where General Prentiss had about 20,000 men.

We were landed, had tents issued to us, and camped on the river bank for several days. No stoves were to be had, and the damp, cold weather made fires a luxury. How to have shelter and warmth at the same time was a puzzle.

Spurred on by the emergency, my thoughts ran very fast, until they were brought to a stop and concentrated upon one idea. All my hunting about the neighborhood failed to result in finding any bricks. Some old pieces lay about, and these were gathered up, together with some old camp kettles. The latter were battered as nearly flat as possible, and then a trench was dug from just inside the front of my tent to and under the rear end. The sides of the trench were built up a few inches, the old kettles placed across, and the whole heaped over with sand. We built a sort of chimney upon the outside end of the long tunnel thus made, and a fire was then started at the inner end of the opening. The draught drew the smoke and heat through the extemporized radiator, and before long we had the sand giving out a very satisfactory degree of warmth. Many pleasant hours were spent in spinning yarns while warming out feet on this product of necessity.

The 47th Indiana was soon ordered away on a campaign, and we were moved into the permanent quarters which they had occupied at Fort Curtis. They had left a portable bakery, all their cooking and heating stoves, as well as many smaller conveniences, and of these we took possession, thus finding compensation for some of our hardships.

It is an unwritten military law—at least it was so decided by our general at the time—that property abandoned in quarters becomes the property of the next occupants, by right of possession.

In about ten days after our removal to the cabin I was awakened one morning by a captain in the regiment recently moved out. He announced the fact that they had returned and were in camp on the hill, about half a mile distant. The courteous manners of the man, my realization of what it then meant to be in a dog-tent without fire, and my confidence in my own ability to find a substitute, induced me to give him my stove, formerly his. A little later he came back with some of his men, and was about to take away all the other stoves and things left behind. The company was turned out under arms to resist, but the warfare was confined to words, and the dispute was settled by the decision mentioned.

It is pertinent to state here that I was in command of my company at the time, owing to the absence of our chief on other duty, and that his promotion shortly after gave me my rank as captain.

When the dispute was settled it again became necessary to find some means of warming my hut. With regrets for having been so good-natured, I set about devising another substitute for a stove. More scraps of bricks could not be found, and stones were as scarce. Finally, an old piece of machinery was discovered, which gave some hopes of success. It was a hollow tube, about two feet long and ten inches in diameter, with a small hole quite close to one of the open ends, and this was planted upright upon the earthen floor of my cabin. We procured an old soup kettle, cut a hole in the bottom for a pipe and capped the cylinder with it; but the question of a stove-pipe was a more serious matter. Not a piece was to be found. The next morning my stove had a pipe, and a fire was merrily burning within the old tube, sending out a heat which made me glad that the stove had been given up. The only trouble with the new arrangement was that one had to lift the pipe and top in order to build or replenish a fire. Sometimes I have a vague impression of some one's having climbed to the top of a distant cabin in the gloom of the night, and when this thought comes to me I seem to see a man standing, in bare feet and scanty clothing, upon the top of that cabin, with the moon trying in vain to secure a good look at him through the thick clouds, and tremble with the fear that he may awaken the sleepers within as he cautiously uplifts their stove-pipe through its hole in the roof. The vision comes like a recollection of a dream, and I often wonder whether the man who secured my stove-pipe for me did not tell me where he got it, and that in so vivid a manner as to leave me with a memory of it like unto that of one who was present.

In February our regiment went with a boat expedition. The object of the trip was unknown to us, but we were stopped by a fort at the head waters of the Yazoo, and returned to camp at Helena after an absence of about forty days. During this time my company was detailed for boat duty up the river, and we had a sharp fight with some rebels on shore, till we landed, drove them off and burned some cabins. No one was seriously hurt. The casualties of the expedition were not large, and the most serious resulted from the guerilla warfare of the rebels along the banks of the rivers, which was finally stopped by landing and burning a few buildings.

We were assigned to provost duty when we returned, and this continued until the latter part of May, when our quarters were moved to the river bank.

Now commenced a system of constant drill

for all the troops, which almost caused a mutiny. Daylight each morning found us in line of battle, and the work was laborious. This was continued till the 4th of July, when the battle of Helena occurred.

This battle is a matter of history, and with its details we have nothing to do in this narrative. Suffice it to say that there is little question in the minds of those who were there as to what saved the day for us. We were, as was usual, in line of battle at daybreak when the attack was made.

The command of our troops was transferred to General Steele soon after the battle, and in September we were moved on the fall campaign to Little Rock, which place was occupied without much trouble, and there we remained for the winter.

Minor skirmishes and battles in which Company B was engaged have not been noticed, as the object is to chronicle only the principal events which led up to the prison life and efforts to escape.

In February we started on the slow march to join Banks at Shreveport, and reached Camden about April 1.

CHAPTER II.

CAPTURED.

Three weeks later our brigade was ordered to escort an empty supply train from Camden to Pine Bluff, and we started on April 22, 1864, about 1300 strong, the force consisting of the 43d Indiana, 36th Iowa, 77th Ohio, one section of the 3d Missouri Battery, and a detachment of the 1st Indiana Cavalry under Major McCauly, the whole commanded by Gen. F. M. Drake, now Governor of Iowa.

Crossing the Washita river, we camped for the night about three miles out. The following two days were Saturday and Sunday, and we advanced little by little, being frequently beset by the enemy, and having constant skirmishing, until about 2 o'clock on Sunday afternoon, when we reached Moro river bottom, and camped until the pioneer corps had completed repairs on the road ahead.

This stream could scarcely be called a river, and yet, when high, it flooded quite a district. At the time of our crossing it was hard to tell where the real channel lay, the whole bottom being one vast marsh, across which was an old corduroy road, or rather a broken line of logs,

some visible and some not. Water was to be seen only in spots, and there was nothing which had even the appearance of a river, but when one stepped off the apology for a road he soon found that the earth was saturated with water, which oozed up like the liquid out of a full sponge when stepped upon.

The teamsters were contrary, and would not move until the road was in a decent condition. They had light wagons, and a little effort on their part would have enabled us to cross over into the Saline bottom that night, when the after-events would have been avoided. But the road was in a bad condition, and it was Sunday afternoon; so we lay there.

Everyone in camp felt a foreboding of evil to come, and when we arose on Monday morning it was with a feeling of keen apprehension and distrust.

We crossed at will, my company being at the head of the second regiment.

On reaching the solid ground beyond the bog we were met by an aid, coming back from the leading regiment, and he called out excitedly to Maj. A. H. Hamilton, who was at the head of our column: "Move your regiment forward, Major, as fast as possible. The rebs have appeared, fully 2000 strong."

We hastened on, and, as we gained the higher ground, the rapid shots of a fierce engagement came to our ears from just over the ridge.

The fight was in the woods, and a hot one. We moved up, and were deployed, but soon all was confusion. The rebels seemed to be everywhere, and, after a brief struggle, it became every man for himself. We had but forty rounds of ammunition with us, and that was soon exhausted, when we learned that we were cut off from our train in the rear.

Sergeant John S. Wood and I were standing near a tree, with Private Jasper Barker between us, and Barker was shot down. We could see that we were largely outnumbered and that there was no well-regulated fight. About twenty-three of the fifty-six men in Company B had been killed or disabled and the rest had no more ammunition. The men on our flanks were melting away by death and retreat, and we finally gave it up and sought safety in the rear; but there was no escape, for we were completely surrounded.

Dodging around, and losing men by capture at every turn, the few of us left at last had to surrender to a little squad under Sergeant Davis. They rode down on us, yelling wildly and flourishing their sabres, but we gave up, with no casualties save the serious injury of Annan L. Silvey, who broke his gun across a tree when called upon to give it up, and who received a sabre stroke for his pains. Most of the others had done the same thing before the rebs came up, when it had been seen that capture was certain.

The sergeant let me keep my sword, but it was taken away later on.

We were marched along toward a corral which the rebels had made for their prisoners, and on the way we had to submit to involuntary trades with our captors for what they chose to give us in return for anything of ours which they saw and fancied.

One fellow made a grab for my hat, but his grasp was eluded with a quick motion and a "No you don't," but the latter remark had scarcely been uttered when an enormous fellow, who wore a big, greasy sombrero with flapping rim, reached out a hand that seemed as large as a small ham, with "By God, Yank, *I* will!"

And he did, his great, broad-rimmed hat being forced down over my ears with a force which made my head ache—at least I think it was the force, but my head ached steadily until that hat had been exchanged for another.

A rebel major came up, and, seeing our captors taking from the prisoners all personal property of value, remonstrated with the offenders, in many cases causing the purloined goods to be returned. He then offered to receive in trust any articles which any officer might see fit to deposit with him for safe keeping, and to give his receipt for them. This offer seemed to be so kind that a general rush was made to take advantage of it, and the major was soon loaded up with a general assortment of personal effects. There can be no doubt as to the safe keeping of the valuables, for they are still in his possession so far as known to the depositors.

The sergeant had not interfered with the promiscuous plundering, but he was inclined to be friendly, and we learned that the force that had captured us was a young army of 7000 mounted infantry that had been sent by Kirby Smith, after his defeat of Banks, to help in the effort to gather in General Steele.

Had we crossed the river on Sunday they would have missed us. As it was, we simply marched right into their open arms, and were enfolded as gracefully and fraternally as could have been expected under the circumstances.

Further talk drew from our captor that he had a mother living in Missouri, where Confederate money was no good, and that he was anxious to send her some greenbacks. Knowing that we were booked for a rebel prison, Davis was enabled to supply his mother with the desired funds by an exchange with some of our boys, who brought forth greenbacks from various hiding places when the object was made known, and the man did us several kindnesses in return. We became quite well acquainted before our separation.

Reaching the corral, or bull pen, as it was more generally called, I recovered from the sorrow and despair which only my efforts to get on the right side of our captors had kept from weighing me down, when I found that it was a most general "round-up." Very few of the command had escaped. Of Company B we counted thirty-five, two of whom were wounded. Nearly all the others had had a similar experience, and it soon became apparent that the proper thing to do was to make the best of a bad job and to watch for a chance to get away.

Company B had ten pairs of brothers on the rolls, of whom eight pairs were separated by death; but we will not dwell upon the dark side of matters. Most of our captors had cloaked their robbery of us with a pretense of trading, but in nearly every case the article offered for exchange was of no comparative value.

Some of us began joking each other about our losses, some accepting the jokes in good part, some being angry, and some too dispirited to care what was going on.

It always has been a principle of mine to look at the bright side of matters, and to find it if none such appeared on the surface. Several others were of the same mind, and we had considerable fun—at least I had—until one of the party began questioning me too closely.

Our lieutenant had bought a horse just before the fight, and in the morning, as we had started on our march, I had offered to give him my watch for the animal. He had agreed to this, and I had then given one of my men, who was marching in his bare feet, an opportunity to ride. Soon after, we had found a pair of boots lying just off the road, and the rider once more had his feet encased in a proper covering. When we had gone into action this man had ridden up and taken his place in the line. Having the horse on my hands, and seeing one of our general's black servants standing behind us, I had turned the horse over to him, giving instructions that he should be kept out of the way of harm. Both horse and rider had disappeared, and had kept out of harm, and further, sight as well. There could be no doubt but what my horse was gone for good, either to the rebels or elsewhere. My claim that the rebels had not taken my watch was soon explained by cross-questioning. When I had to admit this, I suddenly remembered that a friend of mine in one of the other regiments had not shown up, and I went off to look for him. Those fellows had no appreciation of humor, anyway, unless someone else was the object of remarks!

The prisoners were herded together and counted, checked off and then recounted. All the male negroes among our troops and with the train had been killed, and the women and children were huddled in with us.

There had been several citizens with the escort, mostly cotton speculators. Two of the latter, with whom I had talked while en route, were now close to me in the counting, and I learned that one had been forced to give up $140,000 in cash to rebel soldiers, who had traded boots with him and had given him a pair so much too short as to necessitate the cutting out of the toes in order to give room to the toes of his feet. He now stood next to me, the most disconsolate-looking person imaginable, with his long toes sticking out of his boots so far as to enable him to touch the ground with them by slight effort. The other had had $120,000 with him, but had buried it during the fight, marking the spot. As we have no more to do with these men, it may be said here that the latter recovered his money later, going for it under the flag of truce while the dead were being buried.

The only event of the day which had the power to overcome the resolution I had made to be cheerful, despite all the horror and disaster, occurred while we were quietly standing there, awaiting the final count, when we suddenly caught sight of an approaching body of rebels bearing a lot of captured flags, among which I recognized our own, all torn and disfigured as it was, the very scars enabling the recognition.

We can talk lightly of a flag as being only a distinguishing mark or emblem, but its true emblematic character is not realized until some occasion arises to impress upon us what is meant by the flag of our country.

When my gaze rested upon that shot-torn flag

all the memories of its associations flashed through my mind in an instant, as well as the full realization of what its possession would mean to us and what its absence signified. Words cannot express my feelings. I looked around me for a moment, and, meeting the eye of one of our men looking at me, his countenance twitching and his eyes filled with tears, I broke down completely and sobbed like a child for a few minutes.

O ye men, who have only looked upon our country's flag as a pretty emblem! You, who only think of it as a necessary distinguishing mark among nations! And the many who never think of it as anything except a piece of bunting! Be ye once in a position where inability to possess that strip of colored fabric means privation, loss of liberty, separation from home and friends, possibly death, and you will then realize what it means to you as no language can depict!

CHAPTER III.

ON THE MARCH.

After the rebels had paraded and counted us to their entire satisfaction, the prisoners were started on a march to the Washita river. The start was made late in the day, and we were marched fifty-two miles before a halt was ordered on the bank of the river, at a one-wagon ferry, about 4 o'clock the next afternoon. The commander of the forces in charge of the prisoners was a genial, plausible colonel named Hill, who was possessed of a red head and the ability to hold us together by assuring us of our parole when we arrived at our destination. He and his men were very friendly and treated us well; so we marched along, in high hopes of a parole and with excuses for the lack of food during our journey. The prisoners were ferried across the river that night, and we burrowed in the sand on the river bank for sleeping accommodations until morning, but were awakened about 11 o'clock by a call for dinner. We had received nothing to eat up to this time, and had no objections to the hour selected, but we were regaled with cornmeal mush, the quantity apparently being determined upon with a due regard for the supposed ill-effect of too much food in the case of men who were extremely hungry. The negroes who accompanied us were more hungry than we, and the rebels were so careful of them as to give them nothing to eat at this halt.

I found out afterwards that their apparent fear of overloading hungry stomachs developed in an exact proportion to the scarcity of food among the rebels, and it is but justice to say that they exhibited the same regard for their own health that they did for ours.

The next morning we breakfasted upon the memories of our meal of the previous night, and at this time I noticed a pitiful scene. Several negro children, scarcely old enough to talk, were going from fire to fire and poking among the ashes with sticks, their great eyes rolling around at us as if they were committing some depredation. On closer observation, it was found that ears of corn had in some way gotten into the possession of some of us, and that they had been roasted in some of the fires. The children were hunting for the stray kernels of corn left in the ashes, and were greedily eating them when found.

While waiting here for the wagon train to cross the river, several of us went down to bathe. The lack of blankets and clothing among us had been a hardship, and seeing the wagons crossing put an idea into my head. Determining to test the scheme, I took one of my companions with me and hunted around until we found Colonel Hill. He was as busy as a bee, here, there and everywhere, and practically doing all the work himself. Awaiting a favorable moment, we approached him, I assuming a matter-of-fact manner, and, in a business-like way, saying:

"Colonel, our blankets and things are in one of those captured wagons and we need them. Can you not send us under guard to look for them?"

"Certainly, certainly. Here, sergeant, send a couple of men with these gentlemen, to help search the wagons and get their stuff for them," and he was off in a rush to hurry up the crossing of the train.

Two men were detailed to accompany us, with instructions to help us to get our things, and we started.

Going down the road into a strip of woods, and beyond a convenient curve, we waited until a wagon reached us from the ferry boat.

Our guards halted the lumbering vehicle, which was heavily loaded with captured goods of all kinds, and told me to get up and see if I could find our stuff. The driver cursed and swore, but the leveled guns of our escort brought him to terms, and he got down.

I entered the wagon, and found a miscellaneous assortment of personal property, of which

I appropriated all the blankets and clothing, as well as a number of small articles, throwing them out in a heap at the side of the road. In starting the thing my plan had been simply to get some few blankets and a coat or two, but the ready permission and able support had caused me to see the possibilities of the case, and I was now prepared for a wholesale business.

Dismounting, I said to the guards:

"It isn't all here, boys; we had a big lot. These little things we don't want as prisoners, so will just keep the blankets and clothes, and you can have the rest. Here comes the next wagon; there may be more of our stuff in it, so this fellow should be ordered to go on."

The two guards looked at me, then at the heap of plunder, then at each other, and broke into broad grins of appreciation and delight. The driver was ordered to move on, which he finally did, with many oaths and threats, but our escort was now as much interested as we, and we took our pick of the things in several wagons, until twenty blankets and numerous articles of clothing lay piled up beside a heap of small luxuries. We could have plundered the whole train so far as our guards were concerned, but there was a blanket for each two of my men, and, while the wagons were forced on ahead as fast as we finished inspecting them, it was becoming more and more likely that some officer would ride up from the ferry; so we desisted.

One of my appropriations was a very long linen coat, with a huge collar, enormous cuffs, and large flaps over the pockets, a relic of former days. This, and a large Confederate hat, I donned as we returned with our captured goods, and my appearance was the source of much amusement to the boys and wonderment to others. Until this attire was discarded I passed for a citizen prisoner, and many questioning remarks of an amusing character were overheard as I walked to and fro.

Late in the afternoon we were marched about three miles out in the country, and there we camped for the night, being well fed for the first time, but it being the first opportunity of the rebels to feed us well. Our meal was of ash cakes, made of dough rolled in leaves and baked in the ashes of the fires by the negroes. This was the first food given to the negroes with us, and, during the march, I saw a colored woman walking painfully along with a child in her arms and two small ones holding to her skirts, the fear of being killed if they fell behind having kept them up.

The next morning we were separated from the negroes and marched to Camden, which place, in the meantime, had been evacuated by General Steele, reaching there on Saturday morning.

Several days were spent here in arranging for a guard and in registering the prisoners.

The soldiers were all sent to an old cotton

press, and there were robbed of what few things the admirable effort already made in this direction had allowed to remain in their hands, or, rather, concealed in their clothing.

Colonel Polk was provost marshal, and the officers and citizens were taken before him for registration. He asked the names, regiment, etc., of each, entering the replies in a large book. At last he came to a tall, fine-looking fellow, who stood on my right, and this young man gave his name—"J. J. Jennings, 5th Kansas Cavalry."

Colonel Polk laid down his pen and looked up, with a flushed face and swelling veins, blurting out:

"You're one of the d—d gang that burned my house and cleaned out my plantation; I've a notion to hang—no, you're a prisoner. Next!"

He resumed his pen and returned to his writing, but one could see that he harbored much resentment for a legitimate act of warfare which had happened to come home to him.

After we had been duly examined and registered we were sent to the cotton press, where the men were, and here we remained for several days, our promised parole not being forthcoming.

Finally, a sufficient guard was secured, and we were started off for Shreveport, the talk of the parole, having served its purpose, now being forgotten.

The march to Shreveport occupied about a week, and attempts to escape were numerous. Each night several men would get away by having comrades cover them up with leaves so that they would be left behind in the morning. I devised a scheme to capture our guards and liberate ourselves in a body, but most of the men were fearful of failure, and sufficient co-operation could not be secured.

One night, four men dug a hole beside the road and concealed themselves in it, being covered over with leaves and brush. The guards had missed so many by this time that they had resolved to investigate; so, when we had marched just clear of our camp, we were halted, and a couple of officers went back, with drawn swords, and commenced prodding all piles of leaves and likely places of concealment. Soon the point of a sword penetrated through the boughs and leaves over the hole and to the fleshy portion of the anatomy of a man beneath them. A smothered yell and a convulsive spring revealed the place of concealment, and the poor fellows were hauled out and escorted with scant ceremony back to the crowd. Not a man of us but who wished that they had escaped; but the desire to forget our own misery was too great for our sympathy, and the crestfallen men were greeted with shouts, yells, laughter and all sorts of jokes. The guards viewed these attempts good-naturedly, but they had their duty to perform, and their vigilance put a stop to further attempts of this sort. Just before we reached the Red River a young fellow suddenly made a magnificent leap, clearing the fence by the side of the road, and ran like a deer toward a neighboring clump of timber and underbrush. Several shots were fired at him, but he dashed on and gained the timber, two guards following him into it. A short time after the guards came back and said they had killed him, but I afterwards learned of his escape and return to his home.

It is worthy of note that I had become rather popular with our rebel guards, and that by an apparently strange method.

When we were first captured I had made up my mind to make the best of a bad job, and had, therefore, lost no opportunity to be sociable with our captors, while my natural tendencies led me into conversations of raillery and criticism whenever a chance was offered. The desire to forget unpleasant reflections increased both my desire to talk and my ability to do so, and, during the march, I was constantly moving about among the prisoners, interviewing the guards, finding out all I could learn and discussing the situation of the country with every rebel who would talk to me. It had soon become apparent to me that nearly all our guards were not only sociably inclined, but rather disposed to enjoy my comments upon the Confederacy, and the daily talks and discussions, in which I freely gave vent to my ideas, were at once the cause of many fears for my safety, among my comrades, and of increasing popularity among the rebels. The boys held their breath on many occasions, expecting me to be shot for my impudence and candor, reproving me for it as they had a chance; but, whether because the rebels liked criticism, or liked the way in which it was made, I was sought out by them and encouraged in my talks, receiving many tokens of friendship.

One day, as we were wearily plodding along, a strange-looking figure rode up beside me and opened up a conversation. The rider was an ungainly, poorly-dressed, ugly specimen of a country doctor, and his mount was one of the sorriest-looking steeds to be seen in a day's journey among many poor specimens of horseflesh. This man rode along the line, examining the prisoners with an air and look which were gall and wormwood to us. For some reason best known to himself he selected me as his intended victim, and, as he rode up beside me, I was saluted with some remark about d——d Yankees, which brought forth a tirade of raillery from me, in which I expatiated very fully upon stay-at-homes, and negro equality as I knew it to exist in the South. The man was furious, but the several guards within hearing nodded and grinned when I looked toward them, and one of them got close enough to murmur:

"Go it, Yank! Give him h——l!"

The man finally rode off, and I forgot all about the matter, until at noon, when we halted, and one of my fellow-captains came up to me, in a flutter of excitement, and gave me the pleasant intelligence that he had heard them talking of hanging me to the next tree. I did not believe it, and, as the next tree was out of sight ahead, my reception of the information was of a careless nature. It turned out later that the doctor had demanded that I should be hung as one of the blackest-hearted villains he had ever heard talk, and that an investigation had caused him to be sent about his business. This is mentioned as an illustration of the fact that our guards were not looking for chances to shoot prisoners.

We finally reached the Red river, on the bank of which we stood in the rain for over two hours before we were ferried across, and marched through the main street of Shreveport on an old plank road. The whole town turned out to see us, but we were a hard-looking crowd to put on exhibition, yet they halted us for a much longer time than was desirable, while the citizens satisfied their curiosity about Yankee prisoners.

Here I met a rebel major, Lazwell, *from Iowa*.

After our inspection by the natives we were marched beyond the town to a place called Four Mile Springs, where we camped for the night in the rain, and rested as well as we could upon the soil of white clay, which ornamented our persons and showed many evidences of attachment.

When we again started it was with the knowledge that our destination was a stockade at Tyler, Texas, and all hopes vanished save those based upon the prospect of a long imprisonment.

During the march all our boys were constantly regretting that we had made no attempt to escape, and calling themselves idiots for being hoodwinked by the clever Colonel Hill and his talk of parole.

To show the current ideas of Confederate money it will be appropriate to relate an incident of this journey to Tyler:

One day, while we were halted for rest and water, two rebel officers commenced to talk "hoss swap." After each had made a careful examination of the other's horse, one said: "Well, Captain, you'll have to boot me." "All right, Kunnel," said the captain; "how much do you want?" The "kunnel's" answer made me gasp for breath. "Give me a thousand dollars, Captain, and it's a go." "No, that's too much," said the captain; "I will give you five hundred." "All right," said the "kunnel," who evidently thought five hundred "dollars" a small matter of difference in a "hoss swap," "strip your hoss." In the meantime I, with others, had looked the horses over with considerable care and could see but little difference in value between them; they were both very much alike—stout, pony-built sorrels, and in Iowa would have sold for from $75 to $80 in greenbacks.

Just at this time a rebel officer rode by on a beautiful little dapple "dun" pony; he was pacing along at a fine rate, and called forth many expressions of admiration. One of the officers remarked: "The kunnel got a big bargain in that hoss; he done paid only $5000 for him." This horse may have been worth $100 in greenbacks. I had never seen the relative values of the two moneys so well illustrated before.

LIEUTENANT WALTER S. JOHNSON.

CHAPTER IV.

BRIGHT SPOTS.

Lieut. Walter S. Johnson, of Company I, my regiment, now of Lincoln, Neb., was captured with me, and was one of our number on the march from Mark's Mills, Arkansas, the scene of our undoing, to Tyler, Texas. He was afterwards one of my comrades in an attempt to escape. A couple of his experiences are well worthy of record here, and, while one of them occurred during our absence without leave from the stockade, it is related in this chapter because neither incident came to my knowledge until a recent date, and, both being illustrative of kind treatment received, it seems right to place them in a chapter which may be said to be Lieutenant Johnson's, especially as neither of them otherwise needs particular location in my narrative.

The balance of this chapter is to be understood, without quotation marks, as coming from my comrade:

After we had been on our weary march for a number of days, a man came among the prisoners for the purpose of buying up all greenbacks that were for sale. He did not need much help to carry off his purchases, as we had been previously interviewed by others on the same subject, but without the offer to give an equivalent or even the courtesy to ask whether we had a superfluous quantity. This man, therefore, made a favorable impression, and we became curious to learn his object. He was a genteel, unassuming fellow, and spent two or three days with us, talking to individuals as the opportunity offered. At last I asked him why he was giving $5 of Confederate money for one of ours, when he told me frankly that he expected to go to Vicksburg—then within our lines—to buy medicine for the use of their army.

"Do you think it possible to do this?" I asked.

"Oh, yes," he responded; "I have done so several times already, and there is no trouble about it."

In a moment it flashed across my mind that here was a chance to get a letter through to my loved ones at home, and I said to him:

"Would you have the kindness to take a letter through for me and mail it to my wife when you get to Vicksburg?"

"Oh, certainly," he said; "I can do that just as well as not."

With bounding heart I tore a leaf out of my pocket diary and wrote a few lines to my wife, saying that I was all right, telling her to keep up her courage and that all would yet be well.

I gave the precious scrap of paper to the gentleman—without an envelope, as a matter of necessity—*and my wife received it all right* from Vicksburg, where it had been enclosed in an envelope and mailed.

I remember this kind-hearted gentleman with much gratitude, and, as the receipt of the letter would indicate that he got through as expected, the fact has always been to me a source of satisfaction beyond that of personal benefit.

This experience, as well as the one to follow, is recorded all the more readily because the kindnesses received during our sojourn in Rebeldom were not expected, at least by me.

On our return to the stockade, after an escape elsewhere described, an incident occurred which gave me greater faith in human nature than I had possessed up to that time.

We were pretty well used up by our constant traveling, were having little to eat, and I was not feeling very well, perhaps looking even worse than I felt.

Thinking that a cup of milk would be at once a benefit and a positive luxury to me, one morning, just after daylight and before we had broken camp for the day's march under our guards, I made up my mind to visit a house near our resting place and ask for the drink to which my palate had been a stranger for about two years. I was scarcely a presentable object, being barefooted, my pants frayed out up to my knees and hanging in shreds below, my coattails cut off at the waist, my feet wrapped in the detached fragments of my coat, and I wore a white wool hat, given me by the "Johnnies," as the best they had, that drooped so much as to necessitate doubling it up like a "turnover" pie. In this plight I mustered up the courage to present myself at the house, after having secured permission from the guards. Knocking at the door, with some misgivings, I was answered by a sad-looking, yet sweet-faced, middle-aged lady, whose appearance so confused me that I could only stammer my request.

She, with a calm, gentle demeanor, so mother-like that the tears almost started from my eyes, invited me to a seat in a neat and tidy, yet comparatively bare room. This courtesy I acknowledged and declined as respectfully as I knew how, thinking I would only be there a moment. She retired at once to an adjoining room.

The minutes kept slipping away, until I feared that our kind guards would have their patience tried and their suspicions aroused to an extent which would invite an investigation of my whereabouts, especially as we were to move before long. Just as I was beginning to think myself forsaken by the old lady, and was trying to forget the imaginary taste of that expected milk, she reappeared, when, to my surprise and almost consternation, she invited me *to breakfast* with the family in the next room, where the table was ready and bountifully loaded with a substantial meal.

Oh, that breakfast! The sight fairly took my breath for a moment, and I no longer regretted the delay as I feasted my eyes upon the clean and inviting table, with its plentiful supply of creamy biscuit, golden yellow butter, ham and eggs, baked potatoes and steaming coffee; but, as I gazed, even though hungry, worn out and reduced in flesh, a full sense of the kindness exhibited almost caused me to break down utterly and my appetite failed me for the moment. However, my kind hostess, in her gentle, unassuming manner, quietly motioned me to a seat and bade me make myself at home. With the family of four persons I sat at the table throughout the meal. Very few words were spoken. My eyes kept filling with tears and my heart was too full to permit my saying more than "Thank you, and may heaven bless you."

Even at this late day the remembrance of the unpretentious kindness of that dear old lady brings the tears to my eyes.

Such acts in this world of selfishness and coldness are the shade and water in the desert of life, and the longer I live the more I am convinced that nothing short of love for Him in the heart will produce such works.

CHAPTER V.

THE STOCKADE.

In about six days we reached our place of abode, which was about four miles distant from the town of Tyler, in a northeast direction, and on the side of the main road to Marshall. The stockade was called Camp Ford, and was situated in the midst of a section thickly covered with a growth of pine timber, the enclosure consisting of about six or seven acres in a comparatively open space, where the trees had been cut off. The trunks of from one foot to eighteen inches in diameter had been split in two, and cut so that they were about nine feet long. These had been sunk in the ground about three feet and one-half to make the fence around the prison, and the tops of these slabs were about the height of an ordinary man's eyes from the ground.

The enclosure had been recently enlarged, and there were no buildings in it except in the old portion, and these now stood in the northwest corner, where there was a beautiful spring, which gave an abundance of clear and good water.

The stockade had two gates, the main entrance being on the north side and the other through the eastern fence or wall. The guardhouse was opposite the main gate, the headquarters of the rebels in a house over 100 yards down the road toward Tyler, and the hospital about 360 yards beyond.

We stood for over an hour, in all our glory, before the stockade, while the rebels looked us over and checked us off; then we were marched by details into our attractive future home.

My company was directed to the southwest corner of the enclosure, and assigned to quarters consisting of tree stumps, tangled oaks and scrubby pine brush.

Who can adequately describe the feelings which possess a man at such a time!

The remembrance of the patriotic inspiration, and hopes of glory, which actuated the enlistment; the recollection of how the desire for the comforts of life and the pleasures of home associations was suppressed in order that the country's need might be served; feelings of thankfulness that death in battle had not been the result; and then a self-questioning as to whether death would not be preferable to a long, dreary imprisonment; all combine to make one realize the extent of such a misfortune: but a man becomes more miserable when nursing his miseries, and the active employment of mind and body in attempts to remedy present evils is the best means of avoiding depressing influences; so most of us turned our attention to making the best of our situation.

The next morning we held a council, and at once set about laying out a town within the enclosure. Before night the place, if one could have lost sight of the enclosing fence, looked like a very young prairie town. We had regular streets laid out, including a boulevard, and the discussions as to names were as serious as if our town had been a future city. In the southeast corner of the stockade we reserved ground for a public square, where hundreds of men could be seen promenading each pleasant evening. On the south side of this square the sinks were located.

There was an unfinished cabin quite near us, which was partly occupied by old pioneers, and we bought a half interest in the structure. It had two rooms, one low side, and a shed roof. By patching up, one side of this desirable flat was made habitable, and several of us moved in and took possession. We got poles and some oak staves, which sufficed to make rough bunks. Our party consisted of seven officers of the 36th Iowa, and Lieut. John H. Hager, of the 120th New York, who was my berthmate. By the way, I think Lieutenant Hager was the most contented prisoner of the entire lot. He could sleep night and day. Notwithstanding the flies would swarm on him so thick that you could scarcely recognize him, still he would sleep, undisturbed except by sweet dreams.

The ground was staked out for the different companies and allotted to them, all being made as comfortable as possible.

Our party built a porch to our flat, the occupants of the other side joining with us. We got out, under guard, for the purpose of getting the material, and we soon had a protection from the sun before our residences.

I had had malaria for some time before being captured, and a chill every other day for about six months previous to the time of our unwilling visit to the Confederacy, but no chill had I felt since the day of our disaster. Account for it as you will, the facts remain. I was still very weak, however, and our long march had not helped my recovery. I remember that in building the porch to our abode I was scarcely able to carry my share of the brush. While the march had helped to weaken me, the excitement of it had sustained me, but I went to pieces when it was over.

The commander of the stockade at that time was a Colonel Allen, an ex-United States regular, and he was disposed to be as kind as possible to his prisoners. The first protection for the men was such as could be had quickly by throwing up bowers of brush and tree limbs, but Colonel Allen allowed us to go out under guard and cut timber for cabins, and in about six weeks we had completed cabins for all, thus being fairly well housed.

It is needless to say that all the prisoners had the fever of escape, but the chances were very few. Major McCauley, who lived next door to me, succeeded in getting away in a manner which will be spoken of later on.

Our town was soon one of 4000 or 5000 population and built like a Western boom city, avenues and streets being carefully laid off and appropriately named. We had lots of fun in naming some of these streets, and the lots were bought and sold in regulation style. We had a solid business street and efficient police regulations.

Before he left, my friend, Major McCauley, together with Jack Armstrong, a captain in a Kansas colored regiment, and several others, including myself, used to sit under our front porch spinning yarns, devising plans of escape and cracking the backs of a species of bug with a hard shell, which used to be prevalent about our quarters in those days. We planned a good many escapes, but could not hit upon the right method of getting away.

Colonel Allen and his wife were very nice people, and did what they could for us, but it was his business to keep us there, and, while many escaped from the stockade, very few got away.

In policing our enclosure they used a dump cart, which would drive in, be filled with leaves and other litter lying around and then be taken to a ravine outside and dumped.

We conceived the idea of using the cart as a means of escape, and forthwith set about carrying out the scheme. There were some prisoners among us from a Zouave regiment, and one of them was an innocent-looking boy. We enlisted his services, and he soon had the confidence of the cart-driver and was allowed to drive the cart around within the enclosure while it was being loaded. Selecting a favorable opportunity, Major McCauley and Captain Armstrong were laid in the cart and covered with leaves. The major's legs were too long, and, in drawing them within the limits of space allowed, his knees reared themselves so high that, when we had covered them as well as we could, there was very little covering on top. The captain was inclined to be corpulent and was full-blooded, so that, when the leaves covered him, he breathed heavily, and a close observer could notice a regular upheaving of the mass of leaves. We hoped for the best, however, and watched the progress of events with keen interest.

The cart finally started for the exit, and several of us made our way to a good point of observation.

By the time the vehicle had reached the gate the jolting over the rough ground, and the captain's breathing, had settled the leaves until, like the ostrich, the occupants felt secure with their heads covered, but were exposing telltale signs of their presence. McCauley's knees appeared above the leaves like mountain peaks above the timber, while the captain's stomach just showed, like the back of a porpoise above the water as he plunges.

An officer at the gate surveyed the cart, and we expected to see our friends hauled out, but he only smiled grimly and said not a word, while the cart proceeded on its way to the ravine.

We looked at each other in astonishment, and we could see the captain's stomach give an extra heave, evidently with a sigh of relief.

Our astonishment was soon changed to amusement as the officer spurred his horse toward the cart, and then stood quietly by, with a smile on his face, as the driver backed up to the ravine and prepared to dump the cart. A creak, a rush, a cloud of leaves and dust, a glimpse of two tumbling figures, and we saw our friends sitting in the bottom of the ravine, looking up wonderingly at the smiling officer on the bank, who said to them:

"Well, boys, where are you going?"

"To Camp Ford," replied Armstrong; "will you be kind enough to show us the way?"

"Certainly; will you ride or walk?" said the officer, pointing to the waiting cart and the grinning driver.

"Thank you, but we'll walk if it is not too far," was the answer, and the two men limped back to the stockade, good-naturedly smiling at the laughter and jokes which greeted them from such of the inmates as had witnessed the escapade.

For some little time past I had been feeling miserable, my limbs swelling as if with dropsy and my appetite being very poor. I had begun to fear that I was likely to die, when Hiram Pratt, one of the members of my company, proposed a course of treatment which he claimed to have seen used with success in similar cases. After deciding to try his remedy, I was helped to the spring, disrobed and had the cold spring water poured slowly on my back for a few minutes. Almost instantly I felt some relief, and, with a daily repetition of the treatment, I soon became myself again. The cure was so complete that for fourteen months I was entirely free from all signs of the trouble.

Among the many schemes devised for escape from our prison were innumerable tunnel devices, and many of these were planned and worked upon, but nearly all the various workings were discovered in one way or another, and but one was a success, although many men escaped at different times in other ways.

The stockade was full of rumors about probable parole, and these stories, evidently prompted and encouraged by our captors to prevent attempts to escape, kept many of us from risking recapture, and possible death, by uncertain attempts to regain our freedom.

The Fourth of July was soon near at hand, and we asked permission to celebrate the day within the stockade. The consent being given, a number of us went out under guard and cut poles and brush, with which we built a large bower in our public square, as well as a grand stand. When finished we had shelter for over 500, and an enthusiastic crowd gathered about the stand on the Fourth. Colonel Leek had prepared an oration, and Colonel Dugan had written an original poem for the occasion. We applauded both oration and poem; when several speeches were made by those among us who were gifted and inclined that way. Long before we had finished one of the men on the outside of the crowd got so excited that he took off his red shirt and raised it on a pole, amid the cheers, hoots and yells of those about him. Our captors promptly marched a squad of soldiers into the stockade and broke up our gathering, giving as a reason that we had flown the American flag. This was not so. We had several flags among us, but were very careful to keep them out of sight.

While we had several flags, we knew that any display on our part of the stars and stripes would cause appropriation, and we possessed our souls with the knowledge that Old Glory was in no danger while kept in hiding.

CHAPTER VI.

INCIDENTS.

It was the custom of our captors to bring in guards and count us daily. Our town was divided into wards, and the men of each ward fell in at a certain place to be counted, several guards being assigned to each ward to do the counting, which was done by roll-call. We worked this roll-call in various ways to facilitate exchanges, having some man impersonate another who was dead and whose chances of exchange had been good, and covering up escapes by answering to names of those not present. I personally know of one case where a resemblance caused a living man to become dead and buried on the records, while he was carried on the rolls and subsequently exchanged under the name of the man who had actually died. Several men escaped whose names were answered in person afterward by others, who took their place in line and then slipped back to their own places to respond to their own names. In this way a number of men were exchanged under the names of those who had escaped and whose absence had been covered up. This was possible, owing to the roll-call and the few guards who handled large numbers of men, but it was afterwards stopped by a numerical count when a few cases of doubt had occurred.

When the rebels started the new system of counting we used to bother them all we could by causing disappearances. One of the first attempts we made at this was to secrete about 150 men in the lofts and corners of the various buildings which then existed, as well as above the lower weight poles on the roofs of our cabins; the usual custom of hanging blankets to air on the eaves of our quarters enabling us to cover the men who were hidden there.

There was a great excitement and furore when the count showed the shortage and apparent escape. Dogs and searching parties were sent out in all directions without avail, and the next morning it was more excitement when the count was in excess of the required number. We did this constantly, in a small way, although our fun was spoiled after the first large discrepancy, but it served to increase chances of escape by making the rebels pay less attention to a small shortage. They would not attempt to hunt through the stockade for a few men, and after a few cases of finding the missing ones at the next or the following count they could not be sure of an escape until too late to follow with any chance of success.

Exchanges at this time were considerably delayed by the trouble which resulted from the paroles given to the large number of prisoners at Vicksburg. These men were tired of fighting, had no desire to serve the Confederacy again, and not only refrained from again carrying arms against the United States, until regularly exchanged, but sought to avoid doing it at all by keeping out of the way of exchange.

In one of the boat fights on the Red river the rebels captured an army paymaster in citizen's clothes. He was sent to our stockade, was exchanged in due time and sent home, and I learned years after that he had had $150,000 of government money concealed on his person, which he had succeeded in saving and taking back with him.

In this day, when men seem to think it right to get all you can and keep what you get, you will find few like this paymaster.

There were all sorts of trades constantly going on between the prisoners and with outsiders. One of the most amusing scenes I ever witnessed occurred in the case of a farmer who bought a load of assorted truck to sell to the men in the stockade. He had a dilapidated old wagon and a sorry-looking specimen of a mule team, which he drove up to the enclosure and left in charge of his negro boy while he went to headquarters for a guard to escort him inside of our camp and protect him while selling his goods.

The rebels were too busy to give the desired attention to him as soon as he wanted it, and while he was waiting for the detail the guards at the stockade began helping themselves to the contents of his wagon, the negro driver, who was only about fourteen years old, having no ability to prevent the plundering. This made the owner furious, as he witnessed it from a distance, and he came over to the wagon, asking Adjutant McCann for permission to go in without a guard, saying that the prisoners would not steal as much as would the men who should protect him, and expressing his willingness to take his chances alone.

All this conversation was within the hearing of both prisoners and guards, and the adjutant, with a wink at the crowd, ordered the gate guard to permit the passage of the outfit.

A broad grin of satisfaction spread over the faces of all as the large gate swung open, and the crowd of about 500 prisoners that usually stood about the main entrance opened ranks to permit the passage of the wagon, the negro boy driving and his master, with an unmistakable air of triumph, standing erect beside him.

When inside of the enclosure the wagon was driven up our Broadway, the crowd closing in behind and following, and when the merchant and his rig made a stand on Market street he had a crowd of from 1000 to 1500 customers around him, and trade opened up quite briskly, he exchanging his stuff for cash and such available trinkets as were possessed by the boys, putting his own price upon both the goods sold and the articles taken in trade. He was selling out at a rate which caused the money fairly to pour into his hands, and all went smoothly until he made the mistake of raising prices and getting too independent, when his troubles began.

When his talk and manners had given offense to many of the prisoners, and his unjustifiable prices had caused the disapprobation of all, some of the men began slyly to help themselves to small articles. Discovering this, he struck at one of them with his cane, which was snatched from him, whereupon he drew his revolver and swore he would shoot the first man who took anything more.

His lone pistol could not intimidate so large a crowd, and there was something so absurd about the idea that the men laughed in derision, daring him to shoot and promising faithfully to kill him and put him out of his misery if he did.

The poor little negro boy who held the reins was so badly scared that he almost turned white.

After a few exchanges of courtesy, during which the man was so impolitic as to arouse the anger of the crowd at his littleness and bravado, the linch-pins were quietly removed from the axles of his wagon, somebody started his mules, and, in a minute, he and part of his load had been dumped on the ground, amid the yells and shouts of the now excited men, and in less time than it takes to tell it his entire wagon and load had disappeared piecemeal, carried off to various parts of the enclosure and secreted, and he was left standing in the midst of a crowd that had only laughter and sarcasms for his tirade of abuse.

Finally, he became too personal, and then he was violently taken in hand. They took away his revolver, smashed his ancient plug hat, plundered his pockets of his receipts and generally maltreated him.

During the fracas some silver coins were scattered about in the crowd, and a general scramble took place for their possession, during which several heads were ornamented by other than the usual bumps.

When the crowd at last let the merchant depart he was the most bedraggled specimen of humanity that I ever saw.

The guard came in and dispersed the crowd, but there was not enough of his wagon to be found to be of any use, and he slowly and painfully walked out of the enclosure, leading one of his mules, while his boy followed close behind with the other, the master shaking his fist at us and indulging in a forcible, if not elegant, flow of language.

He got more from the boys than his whole outfit was worth before he began to overcharge and put on airs, so that no one felt sorry for him, while all enjoyed the scene of his downfall and spoliation.

After the trader had gotten outside of the stockade the rebel guards took up the matter, joking him severely and laughing at his troubles, consoling him with:

"You can go in without a guard whenever you please. The pris'ners 'lnot steal any more from you than we will!"

Colonel Allen, who, up to this time, had been in charge of our stockade and given us all the attention and comfort possible, was now removed, and a Colonel Borders sent to take care of us. We much regretted the removal of Colonel Allen.

Among the prisoners were a number of steamboat men, who lived by themselves and were called the steamboat squad. They were an unruly crowd and caused much annoyance. The 5th Kansas boys had a row with some of them, and one day the steamboat squad got together and came up to clean out the 5th. At once there was great excitement and we all feared a riot. The leader of the steamboat men was a big Irishman, and his loud-mouthed threats, together with the rough appearance of his crowd, seemed to indicate a hard time for the boys, while no one cared to interfere personally. The 5th was drawn up in line, armed with clubs, to receive the attack; but an officer proposed to settle the dispute by a single stick fight with the steamboat leader, which was hailed with delight by all hands. I do not propose to describe this battle, but everyone who witnessed it was surprised to see the big Irishman receive, in short order, an unmerciful drubbing, which settled what would probably have been a general fight if the two factions had come together; and thus we had some keen excitement to vary the monotony, while disastrous consequences were fortunately avoided by the presence of mind of one man, or, rather, by his skill with the single stick.

CHAPTER VII.

EVENTS.

A noteworthy and impressive feature of our stockade life should not be overlooked. I refer to the religious services held regularly by many of the prisoners. On every Sunday morning a crowd would gather in one corner of the stockade, and men representing numerous religious creeds would meet in unison to worship Him.

Much religious enthusiasm was frequently manifested at these meetings. Many professed conversion, and a number of backsliders were reclaimed. The experiences related by those who had been raised amid Christian influences were particularly interesting. With tears in their eyes men would relate how they had received the parting blessings of pastor, wife, parents and other loved ones, only to come to the army and be surrounded by irreverent comrades. They would tell how hard it had seemed, to be deprived of the help and consolation of regular and customary religious services in the midst of such surroundings, and how much harder the trial had been when the change to prison life had taken place and the separation from home had become total; the recital, an earnest assurance that religious faith was a great consolation in time of adversity, and a stirring appeal to others to have faith that He did all things well, being sufficient to awaken dormant feelings in some, to inspire new thoughts and resolutions in many and to cause all to feel more resigned. No doubt as to the support and consolation afforded by religious faith could have existed in the mind of anyone observing the earnestness and fervor of the leaders in these gatherings.

The religious exercises were not sufficient, however, to suppress the natural inclinations of most of the prisoners to gamble on the slightest provocation; in fact, the confinement and the necessity for doing something to kill time were the means of increasing the ordinary tendencies in this direction.

In ordinary army life it was a common thing, during most any halt, to see "keno" and "chuck-luck" games going on. The halt would scarcely be called before "chuck-luck" boards would begin to appear from knapsacks here and there and rubber ponchos be spread for "keno" games. Five minutes later one could scarcely look in any direction without seeing games of chance in full blast. The prison certainly witnessed more of this in proportion, as the dealers were not reformed in the least, and the gullible ones were as numerous as ever, while the victims of the mania for trying to gain much for little, with the chances all in favor of losing more, were increased by the causes mentioned and from the rebel guards who were allowed to remain within the stockade. After roll-call each morning a dozen or more games would be called in as many different parts of the prison, and an interested crowd would soon be gathered around each game in the open air to watch the betting, which would, at times, cause quite an excitement.

Lieutenant and Adjutant McCann, of the prison guards, always took a lively hand in these games, and he could be seen almost every morning squatting down or sitting flat on the ground, where he could partake of the excitement of "bucking a sure-thing game." One morning, while he was intently engaged in this occupation, some waggish prisoners quietly appropriated his revolvers without his being aware of the transaction; to slip them from the belt being an easy matter when he was in such a posture and so much interested in trying to "break the bank."

When McCann "went broke" himself he left the stockade, still without noticing his loss, but it was not long before he became aware of the theft and indulged in some righteous indignation. He gathered a detail of guards and returned to the stockade, demanding the return of his pistols. Of course, no one had seen them, and not a soul in the enclosure knew anything of them.

The suggestions and remarks, together with

the adjutant's ire on this occasion, made the scene an amusing one, but it soon took a serious turn. One of the prisoners would suggest that the officer had lost his "guns" in the woods before entering the stockade; another would remark that his own men were no better than others, and that some of them had probably "cramped" the weapons; the next would suggest that he might find the pistols in his own quarters if he looked more carefully; and the men kept this up until the officer became nearly frantic with anger. He made numerous threats, but they were insufficient to cause the surrender of the lost revolvers, and no suspicion of any particular parties could well exist under the circumstances, as any one of the 6000 prisoners might have been the malefactor.

The fact that two good revolvers were in the hands of the prisoners was not one calculated to cause indifference on the part of the rebels, as untold trouble might result; so, after a council of war at headquarters, it was decided that cutting off the rations of the entire crowd within the stockade until the missing articles were found would probably inspire the prisoners with better sight, and we were informed that unless the pistols were surrendered within twenty-four hours we should have no more to eat after that time until we discovered and returned the adjutant's armory.

This action was regarded as a "bluff" by the

prisoners, and, after a general discussion, it was decided that our sight could not be improved by such methods; but when we had fasted for twenty-four hours, and the beef and meal wagons had failed to put in an appearance at the regular time, we concluded that the rebels meant business, and it was not long until some-one discovered the lost revolvers, when our guards were advised as to where the weapons could be found.

The surrender of the adjutant's arsenal put an end to an amusing and exciting episode, but it also ended the "keno" and "chuck-luck" games, so far as the guards were concerned, for their commander forbade any of them remaining within the stockade after roll-call. The adjutant never recovered his lost temper—that is, while we knew him, and was a cross officer after this occurrence. Whenever he would enter the stockade, subsequent to his disarmament, some-one would shout "keno," and the cry would be taken up by a thousand voices. This did not help him to forget the revolver incident, and, naturally, did not improve his temper.

"Keno" was also a watchword to notify any-one engaged in tunnel-digging or other contra-band work that it was hazardous to proceed at the time, and by the time any officers or guards entering the stockade could reach any suspected point all unlawful actions would be stopped and any traces covered.

We had a tunnel started in a cabin, the mouth of the hole being sunk in the fireplace. Whenever the watchword, "keno," would sound the digger would hurry out, a false bottom would be set in the fireplace and hurriedly covered with ashes and burning wood, and all evidences of the work effectually hidden from sight.

This tunnel-digging was slow work, as a case-knife was the most effective tool which we possessed, and all the labor of shaping the hole had to be done with this inappropriate implement. Our method of removing the dirt could not be called primitive, inasmuch as the means employed were of neither ancient make nor style, but the device certainly was not of the time-saving kind. A cigar-box, with a string attached, was the vehicle for conveying the dirt from the interior of the works to the surface of the ground, and every ounce of dirt that was loosened by our improvised excavator had to be removed by this apology for a tram car. When the loaded car came to the mouth of the tunnel it was carefully conveyed to some old hole in the neighborhood and there dumped, light dirt sweepings from the ground being scattered over the fresh soil from the tunnel. The lack of speed in the work was offset by the corresponding amount of care that was taken in doing it.

There was every reason in the world for believing that our tunnel would become a success, and it would have done so had it not been for the action of some traitorous prisoner, whose identity never was discovered. This man, whoever he was, had good reason to thank his lucky stars that we were not able to locate him.

Some miserable coward informed the rebels of our work, and, after repeated surveys, they managed to swamp the enterprise, catching the digger, who then happened to be Abel Crow, in the tunnel. Crow was taken outside and made to mark time for hours in the effort to compel his betrayal of the others interested with him in the work. When the guards thought he was about tired out they would question him as to who were his helpers, but he was true blue. He stuttered a good deal under ordinary circumstances, and, when excited, could scarcely be understood by anyone not used to his manner of speech. His uniform reply to the questions asked was:

"M-m-m-my n-n-n-na-na-n-na-name is A-a-a-ab-a-ab-el-Abel Cro-cro-cro-Crow, and I d-d-do-do-don't kn-know anyb-b-bod-y else."

The rebels tried to get this man to say more, and they kept at him until forced to give up the attempt as a bad job, when they complimented him upon his grit and sent him inside without further punishment.

The tunnel had reached fully thirty feet beyond the fence and picket line when the work was stopped, and Abel told one of the guards who were assisting him to mark time during the attempt to learn the names of his co-workers that he could stop work in the tunnel and plainly hear the guard's "One o'clock and all's well," which he knew to be a d———d lie, further informing his listeners that if they had not been in such a d———d big hurry the job would have been finished in about two more days and nights and many of the prisoners would have handed in their resignations.

The statements of Crow to the guard were made in his own stammering way, which must be imagined by the reader, with the assistance of the illustration given of Abel's ability for speech-making, and his combination of frankness and reticence made him no enemies.

Of the disappointment consequent upon the failure of this tunnel to reach the outer world at the proper time and place little need be said. It was only one of many failures, and while the progress made had encouraged a very strong hope, if not expectation, of success, the result was not so exceptional as to cause despair. All who had had confidence in the success of the scheme were naturally a little crestfallen, but we still continued to nourish hopes of a different result in some other case.

ADJUTANT S. K. MAHON.

CHAPTER VIII.

AN ESCAPE.

About the first of August our remaining officers decided that parole or exchange was very unlikely, and we concluded to attempt an escape. Captains Miller and Lambert, with Major Hamilton, had already gone. They had slipped out of the stockade and had finally succeeded in getting home, but the hardships of the journey caused the death of two and nearly killed Hamilton. The result, of course, we did not know at the time, so Captains J. B. Gedney and Thomas M. Fee, Lieutenants Charles Burnbaum and Walter S. Johnson, Adjutant S. K. Mahon and myself made our plans to follow their example.

After considerable diplomatic work we finally closed a deal with one of our guards to secure us an opportunity to get out, for $150 in Confederate money, and he picked out a couple of his companions to help him. We watched and studied the methods of guard-mounting, and selected what seemed to be the most favorable point for our egress. We then informed our friend the guard of the time and place decided upon and instructed him how to have himself and friends fall in at guard-mount, so that they would get the posts which covered our chosen ground.

When the appointed time came we were all nervous and somewhat excited, for we could not tell whether our guards would prove true to us or not, but we were determined, and we made our preparations with the utmost secrecy. We had secured some provisions and an axe, and when we finally started Captain Gedney led the way as pioneer, carrying the axe. I came next, with a pail containing our provisions, on top of which was a large boiled ox heart, and the others followed. As we approached the stockade our hearts beat quickly, and we were in a state of dreadful suspense until we saw that the nearest guard was aware of our presence and found that he was not disposed to see us. We had picked out a spot where the soil was loose, and, when we found that our guard was sincere, it was the work of a very short time to work and separate two slabs of the stockade so that we could squeeze through.

The night was dark and rainy, and fitful flashes of lightning but partly illuminated the scene, yet caused us to crouch close to the ground to avoid discovery. I shall never forget the interval of dread, hope and nervous excitement consequent upon our delay at the fence while forcing an outlet, although it could not have been more than a very few minutes. Between the rumblings of thunder we could hear the low sough and moan of the wind in the trees outside of the stockade, like the suppressed wail of human beings in pain; then would come a flare of flickering lightning through the clouds, like the striking of a match that would not burn, at which we would flatten out against the fence or on the ground, with our hearts in our mouths; then, with the darkness, would come the low roar of distant thunder, like the anathemas of a disappointed match-striker, and we would desperately renew our efforts for fear the successful match would be struck before we got away, our fears being heightened by the evident approach of the worst of the storm. My similes may not be poetic or grand, but it is a fact that it seemed to us as if each flash of lightning was an attempt to find us and each roll of thunder the growls of our captors at the failure.

At last we got through the fence, and at once struck a pace for the woods, which would have carried us to Iowa in short order if we could have kept it up.

We had scarcely started before there came what seemed to me to be the greatest flash of lightning that I had ever seen. For an instant you could have seen to read in the open spot across which we were making all the speed of which we were capable, and then came a yell from one of the guards, the roar of a musket and a rattle of thunder that fairly caused us to become frantic in our efforts to put a proper distance between ourselves and that stockade. In the darkness which followed the glare I plunged head over heels into a small ravine, hugging my bucket of food desperately, but when I arose and hastened on my ox heart had disappeared. We had no time to bewail the loss, however, for our danger of recapture was more serious, and we fairly flew along.

Just what efforts were made to overtake us I do not know, but we finally reached a place where we could hide and take a breathing spell, and no sounds of pursuit disturbed us.

After a time the storm passed over and the moon began to peep through the clouds now and then, when we started again on our journey. The country was what can be best described as an open-timber country, that is, timbered thinly without much underbrush. We walked all night, selecting our course as best as we could, having occasional periods of partial moonlight, then a cloudy spell, and again a thunderstorm. When daylight at last appeared we sought a ravine and a dense thicket and stowed ourselves away.

It cleared off with the rising sun, and we spent the day in hiding, drying our clothes in the sun as best we could. We had no idea where we were, and could only locate directions in a general way; so we talked over the situation and decided to travel by night, going as near north as possible, and to take turns as leader or guide, holding each leader responsible for keeping our course.

When night came it was decided that it was my lead, and I prepared to guide the party north in a country of which I knew nothing, my only support being the consciousness that I knew as much about our surroundings as the others.

We started, and proceeded in a very satisfactory manner until we struck what we took for a bayou. There was a path along the bank, so we turned and followed it for quite a distance, expecting it to lead us to a crossing, but finally concluded that we should wade the stream. I picked out a good place and started in. We walked until tired, sometimes up to our knees in water and again up to our waists, but there seemed to be no other side, and by the time we concluded that we had a swamp to deal with instead of a bayou we knew just about as well how to find the spot we had left as how to reach the other side. After a standing committee of the whole had discussed—and cussed—the situation, in water up to our waists, we decided that it was better to go on than to try retracing our steps, as we would be bound to reach the other side or some side if we only kept on long enough. So I picked out a northerly direction as well as I could and we floundered on.

The silence was not oppressive, as the croaking of innumerable frogs, the buzzing of several million mosquitoes and the splash of the water did not permit such a thing to exist, while exclamations, some partially suppressed and some emphatic, frequently silenced the frogs and startled the mosquitoes, as one or another of the party stepped into a hole or stumbled over a root. At last we struck a place where the water was quite deep, the bottom soft and the bullrushes so thick that we could scarcely wade through them.

When we got where the bullrushes waved over our heads, while the mud was nearly to our knees and the water up to our armpits, the rest of the party stopped and mildly remonstrated, one of them suggesting that my ability as guide was not being displayed in finding the most convenient way to go north, even while I might be going the most direct way, and that there was room for an argument as to whether our most material progress was not toward a place located in another direction.

At this I suggested that as I was their Moses to lead them out of the wilderness I could scarcely be blamed for a visit to my birthplace while the opportunity offered.

Captain Gedney was so exhausted that we were compelled to grope around until we found a place where he could sit down. Before it was found he was so completely fagged out that we had to support him, and, when at last we found where he could sit with his mouth and nose just above water, the situation had become serious.

Then we appointed a committee of one to explore the neighborhood and find, is possible, a place where we could sit down conveniently. Lieutenant Johnson, being the tallest, was selected for this delicate duty, and we rested (!) for a time while he departed on his quest. We had several reports from him in the next few minutes, but they had no bearing upon the object of his mission and are omitted, and then his voice grew fainter and fainter very rapidly. At last we heard him shout to come on, and we went toward his locality in as good order as possible. After some worse floundering than any we had yet had we began to find hard bottom and more shallow water, and in a short time we joined him on a bare space around the roots of a big tree, where we all sat down and awaited daylight, after voting thanks to Johnson for his timely help in the hour of need. We figured out that we must have walked at least ten miles through that swamp, and even today I can hear those frogs and the dismal splash of the water when I allow my mind to dwell upon that night's experience.

Despite our worn-out and exhausted condition, and the drowsy feeling which came to us as the result, we were unable to sleep soundly. The myriads of mosquitoes were not slow to discover our half-stupid condition, and they took a mean advantage of our partial helplessness. I have never been able to decide how much of our exhaustion on the following morning was due to our exertions and how much to the loss of blood which resulted from the attacks of our musical enemies.

CHAPTER IX.

ON THE TRAMP.

With the coming of light we discovered solid ground in the near distance, and we very quickly reached it. Most of our provisions and nearly all our matches had been ruined by the water, so we had a scant breakfast in our wet clothes.

About the time when we finished breakfast we discovered a dog skirmishing about among the brush, and an investigation developed the fact that a colored gentleman was passing by us not very far away. We withdrew to better cover, and I undertook to capture the dog and make friends with him, fearing that otherwise he might discover us to his master.

The capture of the animal was effected with the aid of my suspenders and a few honeyed words, and we quickly became quite friendly, his master loudly calling and whistling for him, while we caressed and fondled him to distract his attention and prevent his barking in reply. When we finally concluded that it was best to get rid of our new companion he was loath to leave us, so Lieutenant Johnson was detailed to lead him off in the swamp and kill him. Just as he was about to start on his mission a deer ran through the woods, quite close to us, and the dog became so excited that we released him, when he at once started on the trail of the deer, and we saw no more of him or his master.

When night came, our clothes had been partially dried by the heat of our bodies and what little sunlight was available, and we started again in high hopes, finding a good road after a short walk. Following this road for an hour or two, we saw a fire ahead of us, and at the same time heard some cattle being driven toward us from the rear. We at once filed out of the road, lying down to await their passing. Just as they got to us a man came riding down the road and headed them off into the woods, and the whole bunch passed right over our bodies, fortunately without stepping upon any of us, although Burnbaum had a very narrow escape; he could have touched the horse ridden by the man. After this incident we concluded to retire for the night, and sought a secluded place, where we made the best beds we could and had a sleep.

In the morning we held a consultation, and decided that we could now travel by daylight if we exercised reasonable caution. Our provisions were now all gone, and we were pretty hungry, so we kept a good lookout for a chance to replenish our larder as we proceeded on our way.

During the day we followed the road, which led us nearly north, avoiding observation by fre-

CAPT. J. B. GEDNEY.

quently taking to the woods and by keeping a skirmisher well ahead to observe all curves in the road. Several cornfields were honored by our making them our headquarters for a time, and we satisfied our hunger and filled up our larder with corn and green watermelons. We made good time, and at night found a good place and slept soundly, having succeeded in getting thoroughly dried.

The next day we resumed our tramp, taking each available opportunity of lolling in the streams of water which we had to cross, thus refreshing ourselves very much.

Seeing a lot of pigs in an open road, near a cornfield, where we had gone for a repast, we vainly sought to catch one. Our affection for those pigs was something moving in its character, at least it kept us moving in a very lively manner for a time. Those pigs were deaf to all our blandishments, and both vigorously and effectually prevented us from embracing what seemed at times to be a good opportunity for a dinner of pork. When it seemed hopeless to expect that any of the animals would listen to reason, Captain Gedney suddenly thought of the axe, which he had laid down until the capture of the pig should have been accomplished. Soon the axe and numerous expletives were being hurled promiscuously at the animals, but his remarks seemed to have no more effect than the axe. All of a sudden the captain changed his tactics, and, instead of hurling the axe first and the wordy missiles after the axe had missed its mark, he savagely directed certain forcible remarks toward an animal that had repeatedly escaped the axe, and then hurled the latter in the same direction. Whether as a result of the preliminary remarks or not, the pig suddenly stopped and looked at his assailant, when the axe, which had previously missed the animal by falling short or passing across his wake, struck him in the loin, and he fell to the ground, a victim of the evil passions of man and his keen appreciation of roast pig.

Our matches had been ruined, and we had become tired of trying to light a fire with the damp articles, but the exigency of this case again caused us to go hopelessly over our stock in a very careful manner. Our joy may be imagined when Lieutenant Mahon found a few stray matches secreted in his vest lining, where, by some mistake, they had escaped a wetting sufficient to ruin them, and we soon had our prize over a fire in a secluded nook, later enjoying such a meal as we had not had in a good while.

The executioner received a vote of thanks for his devotion to our cause, and numerous congratulations upon his proficiency in the art of stopping and killing a pig were showered upon him. He bore his honors meekly, merely remarking that it did him more good to kill that pig than it did to eat him; but while his veracity was never before doubted, the manner in which he devoured his share of that animal, and the quantity which he ate, caused the rest of us to conclude that he found more joy in possession than in pursuit.

Captain Gedney's feet had been troubling him considerably, and the next day we stopped for a rest and to doctor his feet. We used the grease of the pig as a salve, and made him a pair of moccasins out of an old shirt and the tail of his blouse. Late in the day we made a start, and slipped along slowly. Finding no running water, we were forced to drink from pools at the roadside, but we made good progress on our way.

On the seventh day out, as we were marching along through a highly-timbered country that was thickly covered with underbrush, with an extremely hot sun overhead and scarcely a breath of air stirring to relieve the stifling oppression in the atmosphere, Captain Fee had a sunstroke, and we were alarmed, but he quickly recovered and we proceeded.

So far we had seen no one to whom we wanted to speak, and no one not easily avoided.

On the eighth day our few matches had all been used, and our food supply again exhausted. We found some field beans, which we ate raw until we had satisfied our appetites, and then filled our bucket.

We were wearing Confederate shoes made of

poorly-tanned leather, and they had become as hard as iron, wearing off our toenails to the quick and causing us much pain. We had to stop frequently to wrap our toes with rags, and our lack of proper food was beginning to tell upon us, so that our condition was not one to occasion much joyfulness.

On this afternoon we heard the sound of wood-chopping off in the woods, and we went over to investigate, Gedney and myself being appointed as a diplomatic committee to wait upon the unknown parties and see what we could do in the way of negotiating for some provender.

Leaving our companions, we crept slowly and carefully toward the workers, and at last found them to be negroes, a man and a boy, stark naked, whom we surrounded before introducing ourselves.

The result of our mission was that the man directed us where to hide in the bottom, agreeing to come to us after dark and lead us out of the bottom to a better hiding place, when he would secure and bring, as soon as possible, some food to the party from a neighboring house. We conversed with him a short time, and then left to report progress to our comrades and conduct them to the appointed place of meeting.

We waited with considerable impatience and some anxiety until long after the time set by the negro for his coming, and had begun to fear that he was faithless in the matter, when we heard the footsteps of the man and the boy, and they soon appeared, giving as their reason for being so late the fact that they were compelled to cut a certain number of rails that week, and, this being Saturday night, it had been necessary to work quite late to complete their task.

They now led us out of the bottom and secreted us in some underbrush on the high land near the planter's house, then going away to look after our promised provisions, and taking with them the bucket of raw beans which we had carried with us, saying they would have them cooked.

This time we waited until fully 11 P. M., when we became conscious of the approach of several people, and the man soon appeared, followed by a troop of darkeys. They all seemed glad to see us, and had brought us all that we could reasonably have asked. The delay had been caused by stopping to cook some biscuits and steal some sweet potatoes, as well as to boil our bucket of beans. In addition to these luxuries, they had brought us a chicken, cooked with the beans, and they all sat around and talked while we ate a hearty meal, and stowed away what was left for future use.

We now learned for the first time our exact location, and were directed how best to proceed.

Mahon had some spare clothes with him, and we made a requisition upon him for them, that we might trade with our friends for some shoes, which we did. Having no matches, we tried to secure some, but could not. A young negro boy said he could fix us better, and produced a tinder-box made of an old gourd handle and some charred cotton, showing us how to get fire with a flint and a jack-knife. He got fire so easily with it that we were enthusiastic, and at once appointed Captain Fee, at his own earnest request, to be chief of the fire department, the negro boy turning over to him the flint and tinder-box, which he stowed away carefully.

After a long and enjoyable talk with these negroes, during which we became convinced that we could rely upon their people for help whenever we met them, we separated from our friends and went on our way, with light hearts and full stomachs.

CHAPTER X.

RECAPTURED.

Our first objective point after leaving our negro friends was a ferry on the Sulphur Fork of Red River, to which we had been directed by them.

We had reached the plain, direct road to the place, and were journeying along quite happily, in single file, about 2 o'clock A. M. on Sunday, our ninth day out, when we suddenly met and passed a negro man. Our recent experience prompted me to interview him, and my comrades halted in the brush by the roadside while I retraced my steps to overtake the man and learn what we had to expect as we advanced.

He stopped readily as I caught up with him and called out, proving to be a very intelligent darkey, who was on his way home after having been to see his best girl. We had a long and satisfactory talk, and I took him to where my companions were waiting. We found that he was well posted on army matters and the general situation of the country, and he seemed quite anxious to help us all he could, informing us of our near proximity to the ferry, which we might have trouble to cross without help.

By the advice of our new friend, whose name was George, and with his guidance, we removed to a secure hiding place in a ravine, while he agreed to see a friend of his who worked for the ferryman and endeavor to arrange with him for our trip across the river. Our hiding place was perfectly secure against anything except the mosquitoes and gnats, and we were soon discovered by large numbers of these companionable insects. George was to see us again in the afternoon, and we tried to pass away the time by sleeping, but our attempts were not successful. We arranged to sleep in turns, one sitting up to keep off the flies and mosquitoes, but it was more than one could do to keep the tormentors away from his own face and hands; so each of us had to sit up for himself, and sleeping was impossible.

At the appointed time George brought us some food and informed us that we could cross the ferry that night, which we did, his friend ferrying us without charge. The interest of the negroes in us was very great, and they could not do enough for us.

When we left the ferry it was dark and muddy, and we lost our way in the river bottom. After wandering around for a time we blundered into a brier patch and stuck fast in the thorns. The work of our knives, with the assistance of considerable emphatic language, finally released us, and we eventually stumbled into the road again, completely exhausted. Lying down in the mud at the side of the road, we got what sleep we could until daylight dawned.

Our breakfast consisted of biscuits and sow belly, the latter not being remarkable for its freshness.

Proceeding on our way, we came to a huckleberry swamp, into the recesses of which we retired to avoid ferry passengers and to eat our fill of the fruit, which we did at our leisure.

Later in the day we emerged from the swamp and soon came to the high road, which we crossed in a hurry. Coming to a good camping place, we stopped to light a fire and try to cook some sweet potatoes.

Our fire department was called upon to furnish us with a light, and we crowded about him to witness the operation.

The gallant chief produced the apparatus with a confident air, and I loaned him my jackknife for a steel. He held the gourd handle between his knees, as he had seen the negro boy hold it, carefully placing the charred cotton therein, and then, with all the apparent assurance imaginable, he took the flint and steel in his hands, as his instructor had directed, and struck a careless blow with the knife. Not a spark responded to his call, and he looked up at us inquiringly. One of us suggested that it might be necessary to strike a more careful blow on the edge of the flint, and the captain struck such a blow, the result being a shower of sparks that flew all around, but not into the gourd handle. Several more blows followed, with a like result, when three careful attempts were made to catch one of the many sparks which he now had no trouble in producing, the failure causing another inquiring look. I suggested that possibly this was a case for a general alarm and more help, and Johnson hinted delicately that our chief was not sufficiently well trained in his business. These comments caused an invitation to be extended for us to try it ourselves, but we were all modest and declined.

The chief now made one or two more unsuccessful attempts to catch a spark in the cotton, and each effort produced a laugh from us and an inelegant remark from the captain. The expression upon his face and the glare in his eye caused us to move farther away before offering any further advice, when I suggested that he should stop this fooling and strike a light. His reception of my remark was decidedly ungracious, and I retired behind a log, while he made another attempt. This time he caused a spark to alight on the charred cotton, but he forgot to blow it while he looked around with a smile of triumph on his face, and when he looked back at the spark there was none there. The mutterings and suppressed laughter of the rest of us caused the chief to make some emphatic remarks of a lurid nature, and, when I remarked

CAPT. THOMAS M. FEE.

that we would wait while he went back to find the negro boy, he grew furious in his denunciation of such ancient methods of procuring fire. Then I suggested that the potatoes would spoil if he did not hurry up, dodging down behind my log as he looked at me with anything but a loving glance. He now made several careful attempts to locate another spark in the tinder, but history did not repeat itself, and he got up, exclaiming, hoarsely:

"I'll be everlastingly d——d if I know as much as a 10-year-old nigger."

Glaring around him, he caught sight of my head above the log, striving to suppress my laughter enough to utter some words of consolation, when he violently threw the whole fire department at my head, saying:

"Damn you, Swiggett; I suppose I'll never hear the end of this!" and he walked off by himself.

We ate our sweet potatoes raw, as no one cared to risk further failure with the fire apparatus, and after a time our crestfallen chief came back and joined us. Several remarks by the others about the delicacy of baked sweet potatoes were noted by him, and a wild glare at the speakers was the result. I remarked to Captain Gedney that the niggers were very kindly, but that their education was sadly neglected, and that a man who had not as much sense as a

10-year-old negro boy was not a remarkable man.

"You fellows want to let up, or I'll kill some of you," remarked Fee, and then, after the subject had been dropped for a time:

"Say, boys, what will you take to keep mum about this?"

After some bargaining, we finally agreed to keep his experience a secret, and peace was restored; but we had not agreed to drop the matter, and as long as we were together the captain would occasionally see one of us sit down in a confident way and go through a pantomime in which were reproduced his expressions and actions while trying to run our fire department.

The same afternoon, while we were peacefully resting, in seeming security, on the sunny side of the sloping bank of a little creek, we discovered a man on horseback. He was not far off, and carried a gun on his shoulder, being engaged in following the slow trail of a hound, and evidently on our tracks.

We could not run, as he was too near to allow of hope for escape from his gun, and the surrounding country was too open for successful concealment; so we contented ourselves with such protection as the available logs and trees afforded, more because he might shoot when he discovered us than in hope of evading him.

The discovery soon came, when he halted,

gazed upon us with a frightened stare, and screamed out:

"Come, boys; here they are!"

In a moment two other horsemen galloped up, being armed with double-barreled shotguns. They seemed to be worse scared than we were, for their hunt was for runaway negroes, and here they had found six white men, who might be armed.

A deathlike stillness prevailed for some minutes, when it became apparent that they, who were undoubtedly our captors if they wished to be, were afraid of us. Seeing this, I crawled from behind my friendly log and stepped in their direction across the little creek, intending to discuss the matter of letting them go about their business while we went about our own, but the leader suddenly wheeled his horse, brought his gun to a level and commanded me to come no closer. I mildly suggested that an unarmed man could not harm them, but he responded by repeating his command and ordering us under arrest.

Being without weapons, and the situation becoming serious, we had no choice but to submit, for argument was now dangerous.

As we made our captors no trouble, they became comparatively friendly after we had surrendered, and we then learned, as we had before surmised, that they were looking for some runaway negroes. They had found our tracks, where we had slept by the roadside the night before, and in the huckleberry patch, where we had done much foraging, and had seen that one of the tracks showed a shoe much run over at the side, which tallied with that worn by old Ned, one of the escaped darkeys. This track was left by my shoe, and I was at once dubbed "Old Ned" by my companions, Captain Fee remarking that the title was appropriate in several ways.

Despite all our efforts to tell a satisfactory story about ourselves, and to appear careless and independent, our interviewers evidently suspected us to be what we were, and they plied us with questions, finally accusing us of being escaped prisoners, refusing to listen to reason, and ordering us to fall in and move on ahead of them toward the nearest headquarters. Then we pleaded and made all sorts of future promises if they would let us go on about our business, but they were obdurate, and we sadly filed off toward the road, being promised a dose of lead if we tried to run.

Our reflections were now far from pleasant, and for a time we were much depressed, but there was no use of crying, and so we gradually recovered our spirits and hoped for the best.

CHAPTER XI.

THE BACK TRACK.

The location of our recapture was about ten miles from Boston, Texas, and our captors were taking us to that place.

On the way we stopped at a farmhouse to get a drink, and I begged the woman for some thread with which to mend my clothes. She searched around and found a ball, giving me several lengths of thread from it. I then asked her for some patches, and she hunted up a pair of old pants of very small size, evidently a boy's pair. They were corduroy, and it seemed a shame to cut them up, but she said it was all she could do. While she had been gone for the pants I had stolen a ball of thread, which had been left within reach, and I felt some qualms of conscience over it, but necessity had urged me to do it, and I left the matter for necessity to settle with conscience. The pants were carefully stowed away for future use.

Proceeding on our way, we killed time and enlivened our weary tramp by telling stories. One of our captors developed a capacity for lying which was simply astounding. He was not a graceful, elegant liar, telling stories that you might doubt, but could not dispute, but was one of the class of liars who distort facts that are well known and calmly make statements which you know are false. His stories were all upon the subject of eating and big eaters. We stood it until he told a story in which he claimed that he knew a man who had cooked and eaten, at one meal, a rock fish weighing thirty-six pounds, clinching the matter by asserting that he knew it to be a fact, inasmuch as he had seen it done. Then we concluded to shut the mouth of such an egregious and palpable liar.

Burnbaum asked me about my friend down in Baltimore, who was such an enormous eater, and, after some persuasion, I told the following story:

A colored man, called Eating Tom, stopped at a dining stall kept by a widow in Marsh Market one fine morning, and asked the charge for breakfast. The woman kept a table set for twelve, and had provisions cooked and ready for a like number. Being told that twenty-five cents was the price, Tom paid the quarter and took his seat, calling for everything in sight, until he had eaten all the cooked victuals the poor woman had, when he demanded more food or the return of his money, saying that he had paid for his breakfast and had not had enough. At this, the widow began to cry, which attracted the attention of a fat, burly policeman, who ordered the gluttonous brute to leave. Tom and the

CAPT. CHARLES BURNBAUM.

policeman soon got into a dispute as to what constituted a meal, and the negro offered to bet his opponent a guinea that he was yet sufficiently hungry to be able to eat a bundle of hay as large around as the fat policeman's body. The money was put up in my hands, the policeman procured the hay—the nastiest salt marsh hay that he could find—and compressed it to the required size by means of a strap. By this time quite a crowd had gathered. The strap was cut and the hay expanded so that it looked like a wagon-load, but the negro, with a broad grin and without hesitation, commenced his task with apparent relish, and soon ate up every particle of the hay. Being the stakeholder, and an eye-witness, I was compelled to pay over the money to Tom.

Our other two guards saw the point of this story and fairly roared with laughter, but the liar did not seem to appreciate it. However, it accomplished its object, and we heard no more fish or other stories from guard number three while we were together.

We reached Boston about dark and were lodged in a room of the courthouse, on the ground floor, the jail having been recently burned. The town was soon all excitement over our capture, and we had many callers, who were admitted to see and talk with us, while very many more wanted to see us, but could not. We enjoyed a sumptuous meal of bacon and white bread, which was brought to us by citizens, and during our repast we were holding a genuine reception, the citizens taking us in turn and asking many questions about ourselves, the war, our opinions of the situation and future, and, in short, acting as if we were a bureau of information about the outside world. Our guards introduced us, and I heard one of them telling a small crowd about the fish and hay stories. We could not have been treated better if we had been guests instead of prisoners.

Seeing a boy standing near the door and watching us, with his eyes and mouth wide open, I went up to him and asked if he could not go out and get us some buttermilk. He grinned and disappeared like a shot, returning shortly with a quantity of the desired article, and it was keenly relished. Having full stomachs and comfortable quarters, we were all in good humor and laughed and joked with our friends until late at night.

The town was a hard place, and shooting scrapes and rows were numerous, but they were regarded as a matter of course, while our coming was a novelty; so our stay was a source of interest and entertainment to the people, while a matter of good living and comfort to ourselves. Boston was then the county-seat of Union county, but the name did not suit the people, and the title of the county was changed to Davis.

Late at night we retired, making our beds on the soft sides of several bundles of sole leather which were stored in the room, and slept soundly until we were called for breakfast by the guards. This was the first decent sleep we had had since our escape, and we could not have put in our time to better advantage had our resting places been feather beds.

Our breakfast was plentiful and substantial, although plain. The citizens began to gather around before we got started with our meal, and, when we sat down to eat, the room was filled with a curious crowd. Just as we began to eat, the enrolling officer, Captain Payne, came in to see us. He was a typical Southerner, of the long, lean, affable and insincere species, and he approached us with great dignity, rubbing his hands and smiling blandly, exclaiming in an unctuous tone:

"Good morning, gentlemen. I hope your breakfast is satisfactory. What! dry bread! Really, gentlemen, if I had known this before I left my house I would have brought you some molasses. Sorry; very sorry."

Now, molasses was a rare luxury in those days in that section of the country, and I sized the man up in an instant as a smooth liar, who said what he did partly to aggravate us and partly for effect; so I promptly arose and replied, with a bow:

"Captain, your courtesy is overwhelming.

This breakfast stands adjourned until you can send one of these niggers to your house for that molasses."

He turned all colors of the rainbow, and several smothered laughs were heard in the crowd, but he could not well back down, and so we had molasses for breakfast.

The molasses incident seemed to make me popular with many of the rebels, and I was the recipient of many attentions. During the day one of them asked permission to take me out, and our guards permitted me to go in his charge. He took me all over the town, introduced me to many people, insisted upon my getting shaved at his expense, and in every way treated me right royally. Everyone I met seemed curious to learn all he could of the Yankees, and I was questioned and cross-questioned as to all imaginable views of the situation and prospects of the Confederacy. My replies were very frank, and I made no attempt to conceal my thoughts, but they were clothed in good-natured raillery, and my hearers seemed to like my plain speaking. I have very pleasant recollections of that day in Boston, and I scarcely realized that I was a prisoner until it became time for me to return to our quarters.

We had another jolly evening, and it may as well be said here that during our stay of several days in the town we duly entertained scores of callers, from the most aristocratic citizens to the lowest, and were kept in almost constant conversation from early morning until late at night.

The guards were compelled to move the crowd away at times, and then, after having talked to us for hours, we could hear them on the outside of the building, discussing the Yankees and their views, all crediting us with being honest in speaking our sentiments.

The next day it developed that we were likely to be delayed several days, on account of the fact that there was no competent person available to take charge of us and the necessary guard.

During the day we were much entertained by the appearance of an outfit in which we became much interested. An old wagon was driven up and stopped before our quarters, and before long everybody knew all that was to be known about it. The owner was a young man in a Confederate uniform, and he claimed to be a captain on leave of absence because of a wound. One of his feet was bandaged and he limped badly. He said that he belonged to a Georgia company, and had been shot through the ankle in a skirmish. His wagon was loaded with Confederate hats, which he had brought to Boston for sale, and he had a carpet-sack full of Confederate money, while his principal companion was a five-gallon demijohn full of "pine-top" whiskey. A second companion was a negro boy, named Joe, who was evidently very much afraid of his master. The officer and the demijohn were seen to be inseparable, as he kept up a continuous drain upon its capacity for entertainment, the result being that he was as near drunk all the time as a man can be who seems to have no limit to his capacity for stowing away liquor. The efforts of the man to seem entirely sober and business-like, and his evident dependence upon Joe, caused much amusement to all.

In the course of four or five days, during which time our confinement was uncertain as to duration, this young man disposed of his hats, and, professing a desire for such service as he could perform, he volunteered to take charge of the guard which might be detailed to take us back to our prison.

We were not over-anxious to go on, as our stay in Boston had been as pleasant as it could be for prisoners, but this offer was accepted, and the time was fixed for our departure.

After necessary preparation, we made a start for the first station, about thirty miles distant.

On the day following our farewell to Boston we stopped for dinner in an open spot adjoining a farmhouse.

Our friend, the captain, was, as usual, on the verge of being blind drunk, and yet so far from actually being so as to be able to know, in a general sort of way, about what he was doing. While eating our meal our leader learned that I was a Marylander. He swore that I ought to be shot for being a Yankee, and that my comrades were deserving of a like treatment, saying that he would do the job himself if he had not promised to treat us as prisoners of war. I ridiculed the idea of his shooting anybody, especially as several of his prisoners were Masons like himself, and told him that he did not dare to shoot one of them. He swore that they were not Masons whom he would recognize, but that there was his carpet-sack, out of which we could help ourselves to what money we needed.

The negro servant had been sent for a pail of water, and he now returned with it from the nearest farmhouse. The water was not cool enough to suit the captain, and he made the boy throw it out and go for some more. When Joe brought the second supply he received an artistic cursing because he could not bring it quickly enough to avoid a rise in its temperature. Between the bibulous officer and Joe, who was a good-natured fellow, we were provided with considerable amusement during the lunch hour.

During the next afternoon we reached a combined church and schoolhouse, called "Kasseder" by the natives, where was kept a courier station.

The corn which had been wasted in feeding the horses had attracted the hogs owned by the proprietor of the neighboring farmhouse, and they came within a short distance of us, when the captain called for a gun, which was handed to him by one of the guards. The aim of the half-drunken man was very uncertain, and, as the gun was pointed by him in the direction of the hogs, its muzzle swept over a space occupied by several guards and the prisoners, who scattered in a hurry as the threatening instrument swayed to and fro in a hesitating way, at which the officer dropped the gun and laughed boisterously, calling for Joe and his demijohn. Sitting in the door of the church, our inebriated leader interviewed his friend the demijohn, and then ordered Joe to "round up them d——d hogs and shoo them" in his direction, threatening to shoot the first hog that attempted to bite his wounded ankle. Joe laughingly obeyed.

Again partaking of some liquid refreshments, the captain took up the gun, following the hogs in their movements, with an uncertain aim, which again and again caused a scattering among us and much amusement to him. Finally the gun went off in an apparently accidental way, but the finest hog in the lot was killed, and we had roast pork for supper. The farmer did not learn of his loss until one of the guards was sent up to the house to report the death of the hog and ask for some salt. The guards being fearful of punishment for such foraging, the slayer of the animal sent word that we would pay for the hog, but Mr. Floyd, the owner, refused to receive pay, and he furnished the salt to make the pork palatable.

CHAPTER XII.

THE RETURN TO THE STOCKADE.

Our leader had been half sick when he left Boston, and he now became quite ill, soon becoming so much worse that we thought he would die. The drinks which had preceded the killing of the hog had been about the last left in the demijohn, and he had emptied it before the pig was dressed. The march in the intense heat, with the bad whiskey, seemed to have a bad effect, and the next morning we halted to see what the result would be. Seeing that the man would surely die if not relieved, I got permission to hunt up a wagon and take the captain to a doctor, who, as I learned by inquiry, lived a few miles away.

Most of the men were "down upon" their commander, and all were indifferent to his sufferings, simply doing what he asked of them, and that, for the most part, with reluctance.

I got him in the wagon, and, with a guard to accompany me, took him to the doctor, who gave him medicine and got a neighboring farmer to take him into his house.

The sick man stuck to his carpet-sack throughout the trip, and, when he was taken to the house, he had his money with him. After he was put to bed, he pointed to his bank and told me to help myself, seeming to be very grateful for what I had done. Of course, I could not take money for any such service, and he would not have offered it had I not been a prisoner and in a position where the possession of money might avoid much hardship. He told the doctor that he would have died if it had not been for that d——d Yankee, and that he was very glad he had kept his promise by not killing us. He dwelt on the idea that, being a Marylander, I should not have forgotten myself so far as to be found on the wrong side.

We saw no more of the captain, but learned from the doctor that he was improving and would be all right as soon as the effects of the "pine-top" whiskey had been neutralized.

We were delayed for several days, and I got permission to go where I pleased, on the promise that I would not run away.

There was something inviting about the house near our camp, the home of the man named Floyd, whose hog our leader had killed, and one day Captain Fee and I went up to see if we could get some buttermilk. Our personal appearance was not prepossessing, as the entire apparel of each consisted of an old hat, a shirt which was much the worse for wear, a ragged pair of trousers and a well-worn pair of shoes. We had dressed up as well as we could, by washing our faces and hands, before starting for the house, but a modern tramp would have disdained our society, and the young girl who came to the door of the house in response to my knock was inclined to shut the door in our faces. We soon convinced her that we were harmless, and she then invited us to take our seats on the back porch in company with a crippled Confederate soldier, Mrs. Floyd and herself. We spent about half an hour in pleasant conversation, when we made known our errand.

Mrs. Floyd promptly offered to fill our canteens with buttermilk, requesting us to enter the parlor in the meantime and talk to her husband, who was confined to the room by sickness. This we did gladly, and found that Mr. Floyd had been a very sick man, but was now convalescent.

The sick man was quite glad to see us and hear what we had to say. The visit was being enjoyed very much when, looking through the open window, he saw the doctor coming, and advised us to leave the room and not let it be known that we had talked together, the doctor being a very strong Southerner and he a Union man. Accordingly, we slipped out of the back door as the doctor approached the front entrance.

The next day the wounded Confederate soldier came down to our camp with a bundle and a note from the young lady. The bundle contained a couple of shirts, and the note read as follows:

"These two shirts are from a friend, and are to be worn by the two who are the most destitute."

It is perhaps superfluous to add that I appropriated one of the garments, but the shirt was not superfluous.

The next day one of our guards, a boy about fifteen years of age, entered into conversation with me. After talking some time, he invited me to go with him to his father's house for dinner. Securing permission, I went.

His father's name was McMichael, and again I found a Union man, who was forced to be a Confederate or lose all he had in the world. We had a good dinner and an enjoyable chat. I learned that he had three boys in the Confederate service, the youngest, who had given me the invitation to dine, being in the home guard. His daughter was a school-teacher. The wife and this girl ate with us, and all seemed very anxious and joyous to learn of the successes of the Union forces, although the mother's eyes frequently filled with tears as something was said which recalled to her mind the risk run by her boys at the front. I cannot recall the memory of a meal which I enjoyed any better than the one I ate in that old farmhouse with those agreeable people.

While at dinner the parents seemed disturbed

by thoughts of the possibility that their last boy would also be sent to the front, and it was then and there agreed between us that if such should be the case he would desert at the first opportunity and go to my home at Blakesburg, Iowa, where he should attend school until the war was ended. The proposal affected the parents and sister strongly when I made it, and in agreeing to it they united in thanking and blessing me for the happy thought and accompanying offer.

When the time came for me to leave it seemed like a parting with dear friends, and I often recall and see again that dear old lady's face, as, with tears in her eyes, she bade me "Godspeed."

By the time our march was resumed we had become very familiar with our guards, and, in fact, it was more of a picnic excursion than a march of guards with their prisoners.

Each of us slept at night with one of the soldiers, and we went on several midnight expeditions in company. One night we raided a farmhouse and stole a sack of sweet potatoes, sitting up half the night to roast them. Another night we confiscated a beehive and secured some delicious honey. We were continually playing jokes upon each other, and all hands were sorry when the time came to separate.

We fooled along, taking things very easily, and finally reached Camp Ford about thirty days after leaving Boston.

Our reception by the boys in the stockade was

characteristic of men continually seeking to find something to do which would serve to kill time and prevent despondency.

When we were marched up to the gates we were recognized by many in the enclosure, and were hailed by shouts, jeers, sarcastic questionings and all sorts of welcomes.

"How are things up North? How did you leave the folks? Got any mail? Can't you stay awhile?" and many other similar queries were fairly showered upon us.

When we finally entered the enclosure the crowd was drawn up in line, like a lot of hackmen in front of a railroad station in a large city, and, amid much laughter and many jokes, we were hailed with:

"This way to the Palace Hotel!" "Have a cab?" "Cab or carriage, gents?" "*This* way, gents, to the Ebbitt House, the best in the city!"

Our own men gathered about us, and soon dragged us off to our old quarters, where we were plied with question after question, and had to relate all our experiences in detail.

We now took up the stockade life once more, and there was but little variation in its routine.

CHAPTER XIII.

INCIDENTS, AND ANOTHER ESCAPE.

I soon became a stockholder in a tunnel enterprise which was prosecuted vigorously and gave many hopes of success. We started the tunnel inside of an old cabin, using various expedients to conceal the work and get rid of the dirt, all of which were successful. A survey was made to locate the exit in a clump of bushes quite a distance from the stockade, and all was ready for the final move. Quite a number of men were taken into the scheme, and the greatest danger of discovery, that of being "peached" upon by someone on the inside who was more anxious to curry favor with our captors than to be true to his comrades, had been avoided.

The night set for the escape should have been dark, according to calculation, but it turned out to be a clear, starlight night, and some of us were for postponing the enterprise, but the eager spirits prevailed, and the attempt was made. Over a hundred men silently gathered in the neighborhood of the cabin, and the leaders, who had been chosen beforehand, went into the tunnel, followed closely by many others.

A sentinel paced his beat about fifty yards

from the clump of bushes in which our tunnel was to come up, and as he slowly walked up and down, probably thinking of home and friends and wishing for his relief, he was suddenly startled by the sight of several dark forms springing apparently from the bowels of the earth. The tunnel had been miscalculated, and the men emerged several feet from the bushes, in full view of the sentry. He was so astounded that he stood stock still for several minutes without uttering a sound, during which time about fifty men had climbed out of the tunnel and made a streak for liberty. Suddenly the sentry came to his senses, fired his gun, called loudly for the guard, and ran to the mouth of the tunnel, with his bayonet ready for action.

Those who had not entered the tunnel concluded that they did not want to escape that night, and we returned to our quarters in the stockade.

Over fifty got out and away, but the guards put the dogs after them, and nearly all were brought back in the course of a few days.

The most amusing feature of this abortive attempt to escape occurred at the exit of the tunnel after it was blockaded by the sentinel.

The narrow passage was full of men when the bayonet of the sentry prevented further egress, and those inside could not turn back, while none save the leader knew the cause of the halt. The rest were kept in ignorance and suspense until the guards, who quickly gathered around on the outside, had come to their senses and begun to permit the boys to come out of the hole one by one. As the guards would call out, "Next!" and let another unfortunate creep out, only to find himself still a prisoner, the remarks to be heard were decidedly mirth-provoking, even while the situation had its pathetic aspect.

A day or two after this event one of the officers, a captain in another regiment, came to me and asked if I knew where he could get a pair of pants. His own were a sight to behold, and I told him that I had a spare pair with which I did not wish to part, but that I hated to see him in such a plight. He at once offered me some trinkets for them, and proposed to pay me a big value if he ever got back home. I told him that they would be too small for him, and appeared reluctant to sell. A crowd had gathered, as the smallest things were of interest to the prisoners, and when I thought he was sufficiently eager for the trade, I went into our cabin and brought out the pair given to me by the woman whom I had asked for patches while on my return to the stockade. When the pants were produced, and it was seen that they were intended for a small boy, having all conveniences, a shout of laughter went up from the crowd, which brought all the other prisoners in the stockade to see what it meant. The captain was half inclined to be angry at first, but he quickly put his ill-humor aside and joined in the merriment. It is needless to say that the trade was declared off.

A few days later about thirty men of the guard, known as Sweet's men, deserted, and there was trouble in the rebel camp.

The desertion was one of the coolest things I ever saw. This portion of the guard was a cavalry detachment. They had just mounted guard on horseback, about 9 o'clock in the morning, when, apparently by common consent, one man, as leader, gave the signal, and all raised their hats politely, saying, "Good-bye, gentlemen; we are going to Mexico," and rode off. No one dared to follow, as they were well armed.

A new guard was sent, and the balance of the old guard relieved. It was said that these men had been sent to this distant duty on account of doubts as to their loyalty to the Confederacy.

We changed our quarters to a deserted cabin nearer to the gate, and were thereby much better prepared for the coming winter, the move being made because it now seemed certain that we were destined to remain in prison until spring, unless we should be able to effect an escape.

Almost all the prisoners were in need of clothing, and we had been informed that a lot had been shipped to us, but that it was delayed somewhere.

We were all on the lookout for that clothing, and when at last we heard that it had arrived we were joyous until we were informed that, allowing one garment apiece, there would be clothing for only three-fourths of the men. As some men needed shirts, some coats and some pants this promised to be quite a problem to solve, and all the officers were instructed to find out the needs of their men, so as to simplify the matter as much as possible.

When the time came for distribution the clothing allotted to our regiment was turned over to the officers, and we got together to divide it. The men of all the companies except my own were crowding about us and clamoring for what they wanted, but not a man of Company B was on hand. This mute expression of their confidence in my willingness and ability to look out for them was one which I appreciated highly, although they had had several evidences of my willingness and determination to secure for them at least all to which they were entitled.

The number of men not being the same in the different companies, it was hard to divide satisfactorily, and it happened that there was an odd garment of each sort. As the odd men were unequally divided, and fractions were necessarily eliminated, we decided to draw lots for the odd articles. I was the lucky man in the lottery, and Company B had the best of matters.

After the division had been made the neighborhood was a scene of confusion, many quarrels and some fights, until all the clothing had been as fairly distributed as was possible. My company kept away from the crowd and in their own quarters, where I had our allowance conveyed. The men were drawn up in line, and my first sergeant and myself proceeded to allot the garments as seemed most fair. Only one murmur of discontent was heard, and that from a man better clothed than any of his comrades, the men being practically unanimous in their wish that I should decide who needed clothing most and what was most needed.

This incident is related principally to show my appreciation of the conduct of my men, and because I think that I may be pardoned for feeling proud of their confidence in me.

The next three weeks were fully employed by all in making log cabins and in filling up all chinks, as the winter was fast approaching.

During this time I was informed by one of my men that a guard, who had seen me almost every day taking part with the men of my company in some amusement, had been asking questions about me and had sent me word that he wanted to see me. After learning when I could see him, I approached his post at night, when, after he had satisfied himself that I was the right man, he directed the guard on the inside, who was one of the line placed within the stockade when the sentries were doubled each night, to stand aside so that he could talk to me. We leaned against the fence and had a long and interesting

CAPT. J. P. RUMMEL.

conversation, during which he stated that he had frequently noticed the interest manifested by me in my company, and desired to do me a favor because of the attachment he felt for me in consequence, intimating that he was disposed to help me make my escape if I so wished.

Before I left him he had volunteered to let me out, give me a horse, saddle and bridle, inform me as to names and locations of different rebel regiments and furnish me with an expired furlough. I was not inclined to be friendly to the horse idea, although I could see the ease and celerity of my escape if all went well, for I knew that it would be sure death to be discovered as an escaped prisoner with a horse and equipments in my possession; but the guard was so enthusiastic over the matter that I promised to think it over, after thanking him heartily for his kindness.

When I explained the plan to some of my former companions in escape they tried to discourage the idea of escape altogether, saying that we would soon be exchanged, and that another failure would keep us from exchange when the time came. I had no hope of release before the end of the war, and so I sought other companionship, believing that the guard could be induced to help more than one of us.

Capt. J. B. Rummel, of the 120th Ohio, had impressed me as a man of the right sort, and I approached him on the subject. He was ready and willing to try an escape, but he confirmed my own impression about the risk of trying it with horses, and we finally concluded to devise a scheme and try it on foot. He suggested that we take Capt. B. F. Miller, of the same regiment, and we decided to do so, after finding that Miller was as anxious to go as we were to have him do so.

When I saw our friend the guard, he was mad because we would not adopt his scheme, but he showed his desire to help us get away by agreeing to let us out when we got ready, even while insisting that the safest and best way would be to take horses. He said:

"Why, man alive, you can start early in the evening, and the horses will not be missed until late the next day. Then if the stable-door is left open they will not dream that prisoners have taken the horses—at least until you are missed from the stockade. By that time you will be so far away that they can't possibly catch you before you reach the Federal lines on the lower Red River."

I was too timid, however, to risk my life in this way, as I considered the chance of suspicion and apprehension too great, and regarded it as certain death to be caught with a stolen horse. Notwithstanding the risk, I can now see that the guard proposed the plan most likely to insure a successful result.

We determined to try it on foot, but, while we were preparing for a start, another opportunity presented itself, and we took advantage of it rather than risk getting our guard or ourselves into trouble.

Miller, being a turner, manufactured a rude lathe and made numerous articles likely to be purchased, chessmen being the principal of these, being the most salable. We realized some cash from the demand for just such novelties.

Having some flour, we bought some meat on the outside, made some bread, jerked the meat, and thus had provisions and a little money for our enterprise.

We sent out the provisions, little by little, and had them taken to the hospital and concealed until such time as we were ready to start.

Captain Fee was in the hospital at the time, just recovering from an attack of illness, and the day before we were ready to start he came in to see us, on a pass. As we were talking together, I asked to see his pass, and read as follows, on a rough scrap of paper:

"Pass Capt. Fee in and out of stockade, with soap. McCANN, Adjutant."

I was a very good imitator of handwriting, although I had never been guilty of using my gift for unlawful purposes, and, as I read this pass, the manner of our escape was settled, all being fair in war.

After some little effort on my part, Rummel, Miller and myself were each provided with a pass similar to the one on which Fee had been admitted to the stockade. We told no one of our intentions, but decided to leave the next evening, it being understood that I was to go out just before the change of guards at the gate, and that Miller and Rummel should follow a little later, after the change, in order to avoid the presentation of too many passes to one guard.

At the appointed time, after much mental bracing up, I walked quietly to the gate and presented my pass for inspection. The guard looked it over in a hasty manner and silently opened the gate. As I passed out I saw that several hundred men were watching me, and I concluded that in some way our scheme had become known. The colonel and some other officers were sitting on the porch at headquarters when I passed, and I cooly saluted him, saying:

"Good evening, Colonel."

He responded politely, and I walked on to our meeting place at the hospital.

My comrades waited until the guards had been changed, and then, with inward tremor and a bold, confident exterior, they walked in a business-like way to the entrance and submitted their authority for departure, which was duly acknowledged without a question. They soon joined me, in high spirits over the ease with which the departure had been accomplished.

We had $4 in greenbacks between us, and felt quite wealthy. Securing our provisions as soon as darkness came, we quietly slipped over into the woods, thence to the road, and went on our way rejoicing, full of hope and with bright thoughts of home and dear ones.

CHAPTER XIV.

TRAMPS ONCE MORE.

The date of my second escape was the 23d of December, 1864.

We met one solitary horseman in the early part of the night, and we avoided him by having a skirmisher out ahead, who saw the rider in time for us to get out of sight in the woods without being seen, the traveler being a white man, and to be avoided for that reason.

About midnight we met a negro and learned that we were on the Shreveport road instead of the Gilmore road, which latter we wanted to follow. The darkey sized us up correctly in short order, but, as usual with the negroes, the fact that we were escaped prisoners only seemed to make him the more eager to help us, and he asked us if we would not "accommodate" *him* by allowing him to show us a short cut through the woods to the Gilmore road.

We were in a very accommodating mood just then, and we cheerfully allowed him to lead the way. He guided us for what seemed to be a very long distance over a rough piece of wooded country, and finally led us into a broad, well-traveled road and informed us that we were now on the right track.

The darkey was so voluble in his expresssions of gratitude for the honor of being "accommodated" that I had half a notion of presenting him with a bill for services rendered, but we let him off easy by allowing him to thank us profusely, and he seemed to be entirely satisfied, while we did not complain.

We trudged along all night without any incident worthy of mention to break the monotony of our tedious tramp, and at daylight we went off from the road to secure retreat in the woods, and camped for the day.

After a comfortable sleep, we ate sparingly of our provisions and started again at dusk for the North and liberty.

Again we traveled monotonously most of the night, seeing only the stars above us and the weird shadows and forms of silent things about. Occasionally one of us would speak, but it was in a low tone, and only when necessary, for our thoughts were far away, and the solemn stillness of the night impressed us with a keen sense of the danger which at any moment might mean recapture or possibly death.

In the very early hours of the morning we reached the Sabine river and the problem of how to get across. It was dark in the river bottom, but the stream was wide enough to let the starlight and the sheen of the water give a fair amount of illumination on the river.

Miller could not swim, and was afraid to trust to our support; so that means of crossing was out of the question.

We could see a canoe fast to the bank on the opposite side, but we could not call up anyone to bring it over and thus take chances of discovery and betrayal.

Miller would not risk a log, although we explained to him how easily we could push him across upon it. If he could have mounted the log and ridden over it would have been all right, but he would not trust himself in the water unless he had to do so, and we, therefore, retired to the brush for a consultation.

We found a thick clump of trees and bushes just a little way up stream, and pushed our way into them until we stopped in alarm at the greatest racket, it seemed, that we had ever heard. It was a minute or two before we realized what it meant, and then it was all we could do to keep our laughter within proper bounds, despite the fact that we feared the noise about us would alarm the people who, we knew, must be upon the other bank of the river. We had walked into a place which was apparently a roosting spot for all the pigeons in Texas, and our entrance had caused a racket in that still night which would have to be heard to be realized.

We were so startled by the unexpected noise that we were well scared until we learned its cause, and then we quietly stole away to a spot on the river bank where our presence would be no intrusion.

While sitting down, discussing the chances for getting across the river and securing the canoe on the opposite side, Rummel and I drew lots to see who should swim over and borrow it, and the pleasure of so doing was thereby allotted to him. He secured a log, to prevent any accident, straddled it, and in due time reached the canoe and brought it over to us. The carrying capacity of the vessel was limited, and, in fact, it was doubtful whether all three could cross in her at once, but we decided to try it.

Miller was fussy and nervous, as he had had no experience in canoe navigation, and this particular canoe did not have an appearance calculated to inspire confidence in one unused to boats and afraid of the water.

We drew the boat along the bank to a low place, where Rummel and I seated ourselves carefully in the canoe, instructing Miller how to enter and sit down without upsetting our calculations and ourselves, but he was too painstaking and careful. He got both feet into the canoe, but that was all. In being exceedingly careful to place his feet in the proper place he forgot about the perpendicular necessities of the case, and about the time his second foot touched the bottom of the boat his head struck the water.

We reached the bank in safety, pulling Miller after us, but the canoe was then a good distance away.

All desire to censure poor Miller for his awkwardness passed away, as he ruefully asked:

"How in thunder do you expect a man to walk a tight-rope in the dark?"

Remembrances of our own first attempt to keep a canoe under us came to our minds, and the tone in which our friend spoke caused a convulsion of laughter which threatened to betray our presence to any persons within rifle range.

We now drew off to a safe place and built a fire to dry our clothes, a few of our matches, that were in a safe place, not having been entirely ruined.

After we had thoroughly dried out, we recollected our pigeons, and concluded to go back and gather in a few for a feast. It was no trouble to locate them, as they were still keeping up their clatter in a jerky sort of way, partially quieting down for a few minutes and then breaking out again as some disquieted bird would sound a new alarm. The difficulty was to catch some, and we exhausted our ingenuity, patience and vocabulary without being able to bag a pigeon, even though the trees and bushes were fairly loaded with them. Dark as it was, they seemed to see us before we could see them, and would fly away just in time to avoid us, with a total absence of regard for our feelings in the matter.

As the day dawned it turned colder, and a breeze sprang up which had a very prominent "edge" to it.

We discussed the situation, and organized for the coming campaign by electing Rummel as guide of the expedition, Miller as man of all work and myself as minister plenipotentiary and envoy extraordinary for all cases requiring diplomacy.

This day was Christmas, as we discovered by accident, Rummel remarking that he intended to make a note of the date of our baptism, and asking what day of the month it was.

There was no Christmas for us, however, and we banished all thoughts of roast turkey or pigeons and of home comforts by taking up the all-absorbing question of how to cross the river.

Rummel suggested that Miller should be made to cross on a log in tow of ourselves, inasmuch as he had shown a greater fondness for the water than he had professed, but we decided to walk a short distance up stream in an effort to find a ford before trying to swim the river.

About half a mile beyond the scene of our upset we found a riffle, and I was appointed to investigate the character of the bottom and find the best place to cross.

Divesting myself of my clothes, and leaving

them to be brought over by my companions after I should have picked out a course for them, I entered the cold water and proceeded to investigate. At almost the first step I slipped from a smooth rock into a pool and went in over my head. As I came up, Miller remarked that I need make no report on that locality, and I tried a little farther down. This time I struck a straight course in a depth varying from my knees to my armpits, and reached the opposite shore, after a struggle to keep my feet at the points where the water was deepest.

When I emerged from the water the keen wind nearly took my breath away, as its cold was made more intense by my recent immersion. Hastily getting under the lee of a big tree on the bank, I shouted for my companions to come over, and be lively about it, but they were engaged in a discussion, and I could see that Miller was hanging back.

My teeth were now chattering and I was shaking as if with the ague; so I yelled spasmodically to Rummel to come on and bring my clothes if he did not want to see me lose all my teeth.

Rummel undressed and started, carrying his clothes and mine above his head, and Miller followed when he saw that he was to be left behind. Both got over in safety and without wetting the clothing, but I was so cold when they arrived that it took over an hour for me to get over my shivering fit.

Captain Miller was in many respects one of the finest characters I ever knew, and I liked him more as I knew more of him, but he was the most apprehensive individual imaginable. He was more afraid of a river than of the whole Confederate army, and was continually imagining all sorts of possible contingencies, trying to decide in advance what was to be done in each case, and losing sight of the fact that we could not foresee any of the surrounding conditions of a probable contingency, and hence could not meet the emergency until it and all its phases could be clearly seen. He bothered me half to death at times by his questions as to what I would do if such and such a thing occurred, and when I told him that I could not tell until it happened he would look as serious as if we were in immediate danger.

I never could make a success of trying to anticipate details, for I always found that my action turned upon some unforeseen thing, and I never worried about such things, having found that the proper action for an emergency always suggested itself to me when I stood face to face with the necessity for doing something.

As we proceeded on our way we came to a bayou, which we waded, and a little later we reached one which was too deep to be forded. We seemed to be in a section cut up by a network of these streams, and we concluded that by a little extra walking we could probably dodge around bends in the streams so as to preserve our general course without recourse to the swimming which Miller so dreaded. We could see no signs of a curve in this bayou, and it was a question of luck as to whether we went right or wrong in our first attempt to get around the obstruction.

Rummel was our guide, and we would have followed his lead had he started off, but he hesitated so long, and did so much guessing, that I started off to the left, saying that one way was as good as the other when we had nothing to point out the best course. Of course, Miller now wanted to go the other way, and we came as near having a row as we ever did in all our acquaintance. After some sarcasm and heated comments, we started off, finally, in the direction which I had chosen, and a few minutes' walking proved that I had by accident chosen correctly, as we saw a curve ahead of us which subsequently proved to be a bend in the bayou. Our passage around the curve opened up a good stretch of country ahead of us, and I could not help reminding Miller that we had lost more time in discussion than it would have taken to prove the case one way or the other. This was our only dispute, and it was not serious.

CHAPTER XV.

DIPLOMACY.

We had a rubber poncho and three blankets with us, and the country through which we had passed had seemed so sparsely settled that we were traveling by day and sleeping at night, getting our scarce and poor food as occasion offered and living upon anything but a generous diet.

About dusk on the day of our little difference we were looking for a safe place to camp, when we saw the figure of a man on the opposite side of an open space. He was evidently surveying us intently, as he stood stock still, and his appearance was not rendered more attractive to us by the fact that he held a gun in the hollow of his left arm.

We sank gracefully to the ground and waited for some hail which would announce to us the intentions of our friend. None coming, we concluded that he was as much afraid of us as we were of him, and I crawled to a spot where I could see, without rising, what had become of him. He still stood there, evidently awaiting our next move, and I slunk back to my companions.

We decided that the quickest way to learn who and what he was would be to approach him, and that he certainly would not shoot if we held up our hands. Accordingly we stood up, held up our hands, and stepped boldly out into the clearing, I calling out:

"We are unarmed and are friends."

Not a move did he make, but we fancied we could see the gun move a little, and we quickly halted, Rummel exclaiming:

"Don't shoot! we are unarmed and peaceable citizens."

As he said this, Miller burst into a loud laugh, and quickly ran toward the figure. We instantly comprehended the situation and followed him, arriving at the fantastic stump of a burned tree, to be saluted by Miller with:

"Would you unarmed and peaceable citizens kindly recollect this event when you are inclined to joke me about that canoe?"

We had nothing to say.

The next day we met a negro, who gave us our course for Dangerfield, describing a corner of the square in the town, from which a plain road led to a ferry across the Sulphur Fork of Red River.

This was the 27th of December, and we reached the outskirts of the town late in the afternoon, hiding in some bushes until night.

When it was late enough we started boldly

through the town, found the corner described, and took the road at a rapid gait.

Just as the east was beginning to show signs of approaching day we struck what we took to be another bayou.

Miller was anxious to show that he could brave the water in some cases, so he pulled off his pants, handed them to me for safe keeping, and started right in to wade the stream. He took two steps and disappeared from view. We fished him out and concluded that we would wait for daylight before proceeding farther.

When day broke we found that we must have made better time from Dangerfield than we had expected, for this was certainly a river, and could be no other than Sulphur Fork. It was high, and running swiftly in the middle, the water being far above the banks and out into the woods on both sides, so that it must have been fully two miles and one-half across. No signs of a ferry were to be seen, and we hunted a good place for a camp in which to lay over until the river should subside or something turn up to decide us as to a way of crossing.

In building a fire I strained my instep by kicking a limb from a log, and it became quite sore before the day was over.

The next day the river was as high as ever, and my foot was so sore that I could scarcely step upon it. We lay over all day, as I could not walk, and there seemed to be no prospect of crossing the turbulent stream.

On the following morning my foot was much swollen, but I could limp around, and the river seemed to be falling, so I insisted upon some action, and started off to look around a little, leaving my companions to await my return. They both wanted to go in my place, but we agreed that it was best for me to go, so far as the chance of having to deal with an emergency was concerned.

I hunted around for a while, but found nothing, and returned to my companions. Just as I reached them we heard a pounding in the opposite direction from which I had gone.

Kummel sneaked off, and soon returned with the report that he had seen a horse a short distance down the road.

Again I started to investigate our surroundings. The horse was soon found. He was hobbled, and close to him, in the woods, were two others. It was a certainty that we had neighbors, but I could see nothing of them, and, concluding that the owners had gone down to the river, I walked boldly toward the animals to discover by their trappings what I could about the riders. I had not proceeded more than a few yards before I came to a thick clump of bushes, and, in skirting around the edge of them, almost stumbled over three rebel soldiers, who were stretched out comfortably on their blankets for a nap.

They looked up inquiringly at me as I suddenly halted and gave involuntary utterance to an exclamation of surprise.

To say that I was scared would but feebly express my feelings. The cold chills ran up and down my back, and I could not speak for an instant. However, I quickly recovered myself, before they had a chance to speak, and said to them:

"Hello, boys! I knew you were somewhere about, for I saw your horses and was looking for you, but I was not expecting to find you so near at hand, and I must confess that you startled me. How can a fellow get across this infernal river?"

They informed me that they had been pounding to attract the attention of the ferryman, who was on the other side, but they could not get near the river bank, and could not see the ferryboat, so had concluded to take a nap.

Without giving them time to question me, I plied them with questions, which developed the fact that they were members of General Gano's command, and were despatch-bearers from Kirby Smith to General Magruder. They expressed a strong desire to cross the river in a hurry, and threatened to take forcible possession of the boat if the ferryman did not make another trip that afternoon.

I then informed them that two comrades were with me, that they were in camp a short distance back from the river, that we would join in capturing the ferry-boat, and that if they had no objections to offer I would go up and get the boys, so that we could cross and travel together.

They told me to go ahead and I went; but, after walking easily along until out of sight in the opposite direction from where my companions were I broke into a run, skirted around through the woods, joined Rummel and Miller, told them the facts, and we at once broke camp, running around the river bank a mile or more, and secreting ourselves on the top of the bank in a thick clump of bushes and timber, right alongside of the road, where they would not be likely to look for us if they wondered at my failure to return.

From the moment when my eyes had rested upon the figures of those three soldiers I had forgotten my sore foot altogether, and never felt it during my run and our subsequent movements. The strangest part of this incident of my injured foot is the fact that I never afterward felt soreness or a twinge of pain in it. I leave it for others to explain. I simply state the facts.

After we had settled down in our hiding place we saw a number of people coming up the road, evidently from the ferry, and our three soldiers were among them. From their talk as they passed us we gathered that the ferry-boat had come over, but would not go back again before morning, and we concluded that the three soldiers were going to some place to stay over night.

After these people had passed, I set out to hunt up some negro who could help us get over the river. As I crossed the road I saw a darkey driving a wagon toward the ferry, and I stopped to speak to him. Before I had a chance to say more than a few words the man's master rode into view, and I had to go on talking to avoid casting suspicion by sudden disappearance.

When the master rode up I talked with him, telling him what I had told the soldiers, and saying that we had given up seeing the boat until we had seen the people coming up from the ferry, when I had left my friends, to see if we could cross that evening.

We all traveled down the road together, and the negro's master showed me where the ferryman lived, a little way off the road, and went up to the house with me. He and the ferryman were acquainted, and, while they talked, I went coolly up on the piazza of the house and sat down, turning over in my mind the question of what I should tell that ferryman.

If I stuck to my story, as told to the soldiers, I had no excuse for a special crossing, which I wanted to urge, and we should run great risk of discovery if we waited and crossed with the others. As I studied the face of the ferryman I decided upon my course of action, and when the old gentleman who was talking to him had left to arrange for the care of his wagon and animals for the night I gave the ferryman no chance to think or question, but took him around to the side of the house, where we could not be overheard by anyone in the building, and transfixed him by saying:

"I am an escaped Yankee prisoner from Camp Ford, Texas, and have been water-bound on the river for two days. I have come to have you either ferry me over the river or capture me."

The man seemed to be dumbfounded, and he stared at me in perfect amazement, without speaking a word.

I told him that I had no honeyed promises to make, that the only inducement there had been for me to attempt such a hazardous trip in the dead of winter was my intense longing to see my wife and children in Iowa, who did not know whether I was alive or dead, and had not known since my capture on the 25th of the previous April, and that, after seeing them, I expected to return to my regiment and remain until the war ended, if I was not sooner killed. Keeping up this line of conversation, I completely magnetized the ferryman, either by my nerve or the apparent confidence I had in his disposition to let his humanity instead of war's inhumanity control his actions.

The first words uttered by him were:

"Well, all I ask is for you to pay your fare and take your chances. The boat is loaded at each trip, and you may be suspected by the passengers. The fare is five dollars in Confederate, or a dollar and a-half in Federal money."

After he had recovered from his surprise sufficiently to agree to this, I told him that I had two companions with me, when he exclaimed:

"Oh, h——l! But d——d if I don't help you fellows anyhow. I can't understand why I agreed to help you, for I'm as rank a rebel as they make, and if I am caught at it, and you give me away, I'll be shot, sure as h——l."

I promptly declared that I would submit to being hung myself before I would give him away, and this seemed fully to reconcile him to his undertaking, for he replied:

"D——d if I don't believe you, young man."

We had but $4 in greenbacks, which I told him, together with the fact that we wanted some bread, and we compromised by my giving him $3 for our fare across the river and $1 for a supply of corn bread.

He would not make a special trip that night, as it might get him into trouble if we were discovered, but he agreed to put us over the river in the morning, do the best he could for us, and keep his mouth shut about us.

I returned to my companions to report progress, and it would have been hard to find two happier men than Rummel and Miller; they were simply delighted with the result of my mission.

After a meal upon the corn bread bought from the ferryman, we turned in for the night.

CHAPTER XVI.

MAKING PROGRESS.

At an early hour the next morning we were on hand at the boatman's house.

When we reached the boat we found our friend with the wagon and negro driver, together with several other parties, already there, and I was much relieved to see that the three soldiers had not arrived.

The ferryman told us to go to the bow of the boat and avoid questioning, which we did.

Just as we had shoved off, and were being hauled along through the trees to the river bank where the ferry wire was tied, we heard a shout, and, looking back, saw three horsemen approaching on a gallop. The ferryman did not stop, and one of the riders yelled out fiercely, and fired his gun to show that they would make us stop if we did not choose to do so, whereupon the boat was stopped and slowly pushed back to the water's edge.

Our relief can be imagined when I discovered that the riders were not our soldier friends.

As we emerged from the trees into the river channel the current was very strong, and the heavy load seemed too much for the ferryman and his helper.

This helper was an old man of an inquisitive nature and appearance, and I was afraid that he might say or ask something which would attract more attention to us than was necessary for our comfort or desire for prominence; so I got up and went over to him, taking hold of the rope and helping him with the boat, while I plied him with questions so thick and fast that he only got the opportunity to ask me two questions, both of which were easily answered.

As we reached the farther shore we had to pull and push the boat among the trees for nearly half a mile before we reached the ground, and my old friend was anxious that my friends and myself should be assisted over the marshy bottom, which extended for some distance, by riding behind the three horsemen.

He proposed this to the riders, but the visible reluctance of these gentlemen enabled me to get out of this disagreeable situation with credit to ourselves, and we struck off through the swamp on our own hook, after hearing the following remark of the ferryman, made as one of the riders offered to pay him with a $5 bill of an issue which the Confederacy had recalled, with a notice that they would not be redeemed by exchange or otherwise after the coming 1st of January:

"My God, man! I would as soon have a notch on one of them trees as one of them bills."

After a short walk through the swampy bottom, we struck what was then an island, and on which were camped about 150 refugees from Missouri. They had their live stock and all belongings with them.

These people had been too friendly to the South, when Price was in their State, to make it healthy there for them after he had been driven out, and they had come to Texas and were living as best they could. From them we learned that Price's army was at Spring Hill, and we told them that we were members of his "walking company," as the rebels called Price's infantry.

As our feet were wet from our walk through the marsh, we got away from this crowd as soon as possible and went over to the camp of an old woman for the purpose of getting permission to dry our clothes and shoes. The favor was ganted on application, and we sat there chatting with the woman and her sons until we were thoroughly dried out. During this talk we learned that these refugees were disposed to be quite bitter toward the Texans for the lack of sympathy and hospitality which they thought should be forthcoming on account of the abuse and persecution which they had suffered for their Southern sympathies.

After we had dried ourselves sufficiently, we

borrowed a brand from the fire and went off to make a camp of our own.

On our way to a choice spot we met a sick soldier, who was on a furlough and who had a canoe. He offered to take us with him across the balance of the swamp, but we declined, because we did not wish to cultivate his acquaintance and because of our friend Miller.

We waded into the swamp and went at least a mile before we found dry land, when we picked out a secluded spot, lit a fire and again dried ourselves thoroughly, going off to some tangled oaks for a sleep while we waited for night.

Our location was now about ten miles from Boston, and I knew the road; so we dozed off, in the confidence of apparent security.

I was awakened by a sound which startled me, and as I listened, it proved to be a rustle in the underbrush, heard at intervals, and the sound of a bell. The others were called by me, and we hid more securely, as the footsteps of a man were now to be heard. Soon we saw a most cadaverous, tall and poverty-stricken looking individual approaching in an erratic manner, and we could now hear his low-toned mutterings as he darted here and there. As the lower portion of his body came into view we saw that he was driving an old sow, with a bell attached to her neck, and that he carried an old rifle, with its stock tied on with strings. He seemed to be one of the refugees who had been after his stray hog, and we arose from our concealment and approached him.

He was literally dressed in rags, and was inclined to be scared at our appearance, but we soon pacified him, and had an interesting conversation, during which we learned his whole history.

The interest in this incident exists in the fact that, although I had seen many Southern men with Northern sympathies, this was the first out and out rebel I had seen who talked "lost cause."

When night came, we made our way to Boston and passed through the town in the silence of the deserted streets, the hour being that of very early morn. The fact that I had spent so many days here, after having been recaptured on my previous runaway trip, made the spot interesting to both my companions and myself, and I pointed out to them all the various points of note. Had we had any chalk with us I should certainly have left my card, in the shape of some notes, on various doors; but, as it was, we passed through and on. We went about five miles beyond the town and camped for the day.

The next night we proceeded without interruption or incident worthy of note, and reached a deserted cabin about daylight, in which we slept soundly all day, lying on a few boards in the loft, close to the eaves, where we were securely hidden. The hut had been used by sheep for shelter, and it was not excessively clean, but the weather was cold and threatening when we turned in, and we were not sticklers about trifles like that.

Our pants were all wet from crossing "slues" and watercourses during the night, and we were too tired to sit up and dry them out before going to sleep. When we awoke they were frozen stiff and we were chilled through.

I was awakened by hearing a woman singing as she passed by the old hut, and as we lay there, rubbing our limbs to restore the circulation, we heard a splashing and squealing near the hut, which had awakened my companions and now caused me to go outside to investigate, when it was found that an enormous rat had tumbled into an old, abandoned well at the corner of the house. We put him out of his misery and took a run down a ravine, where we built a good fire and got thoroughly warmed up.

After a scanty meal, we again took to the road and tramped all night, meeting with no mishaps and making good progress.

In the morning we profited by experience, and went into a ravine, built a fire and dried out before turning in for the day.

The next night we came to a bayou, about 11 o'clock, and crossed on logs. Finding a bad road beyond, we sought a retired spot and turned in to wait for daylight.

In the morning we skirmished around for something to eat, and found it in the cabin of an old negro, whom we nearly scared to death as we took possession of his hut. From him we learned that we were in the Red River bottom, and he directed us how to proceed on our course, telling us to turn to the right at a certain point, which he described.

After eating heartily of our corn bread and sow belly, we started off in high spirits, and soon found the spot where we were to turn to the right, which direction we followed out until the road turned into a cow-path and finally led us to the bars of a fence across the road at the edge of a thick wood.

We knew that we were lost and had come a long distance since taking the right (?) direction. Knowing that we had obeyed the instructions given us, we were inclined to be wrathy, and we sat down for greater ease and support while we cussed that nigger "up hill and down." Rummel and I did the cussing, while Miller watched for a chance to break in upon our monopoly of the conversation, when he mildly suggested that, as the nigger was standing with his face to us when he told us how to proceed, and as we were facing in the direction which we were to take, it was likely that the darkey had meant his right and not ours, which plausible explanation only made us the more wrathy, because the nigger had been stupid instead of having willfully misled us, as we had taken it for granted he had.

When we had vented our spleen and rested up, we struck out, at a venture, in preference to retracing our steps. After a tedious struggle through the underbrush and a thorough wetting in the bayou we had to cross we at length came upon a large field in which about 100 negroes were burning stumps and clearing ground. Selecting a hiding place, we lay in wait to single out some darkey who could be entrusted with our management until we could cross the Red River and again get started on our way.

After some little time spent in a study of the various faces which came near enough to be seen plainly, I selected two men who walked together and seemed to be brothers. It took a good deal of patience to await a chance to see them alone, and we talked over all sorts of schemes for securing a private interview with these darkeys. About the time when we gave up all scheming and decided to trust to chance, the question was settled for us by the two men starting off in our direction, with an evident intention of leaving the field.

In my capacity of diplomat I was sent to waylay them at a proper spot and negotiate for what we needed in the way of food and assistance. By a little manoeuvring the darkeys were intercepted at a suitable spot, and I found them to be very intelligent men, who were only too glad to help us all they could. They were slaves on a plantation located on the banks of the Red

River, of which the field was a portion, and they were on their way to the outbuildings, near at hand, for some tools. They left me, to get the articles needed in the field, and soon returned, bringing with them a liberal portion of their day's allowance of food, which they gave to me. Before returning to the field they gave me explicit directions how to find the river bank after night at the proper place, where they agreed to meet us and set us across the river. They gave their names as Taylor and Sam Jeans, and promised to bring us some more provisions when they met us as agreed.

I returned to Rummel and Miller, and we had a hearty meal, watching the negroes at work while we ate, and continuing to watch them until they quit work and went home.

CHAPTER XVII.

A PUZZLE, AND INCIDENTS.

When the appointed time drew near we broke camp and proceeded to the designated spot on the river bank, which we found without much trouble. We waited and waited, but no negroes appeared. It was now nearly midnight, and a bright moon began to illuminate our surroundings with the ghostly light that proceeds from a combination of the moon's rays with the darkness and shadows of a timbered river bottom. We waited until we could no longer hear a sound from the plantation houses in the distance and for at least an hour after total silence reigned all about us. Then we began to fear that the negroes had forgotten us, and I was despatched to see what I could find.

Now comes a part of my story which I must leave to wiser heads than mine for explanation. I simply state the facts as they occurred and leave the reader to satisfy himself or herself as to the controlling influence which prompted my actions. I cannot satisfactorily explain them to myself.

I did not know a single foot of the ground over which I was to travel, and my only guide as to where I wanted to go was the remembrance of the direction in which we had heard the sounds of plantation life in the early evening.

I started off through a field and came upon a narrow road on the other side, evidently a cross road. Down this I turned, in a direction which did not accord with my memory of the proper course, and yet I seemed to be impelled that way. I soon came to a turnstile in the fence on one side, and through this I passed without a moment's hesitation, although there was nothing in sight except a narrow path. Some distance down the path I came to a double row of negro cabins, about twenty on each side of a narrow street, facing each other. I did not know what I was to do, and to find a particular negro in that array of cabins without arousing the whole outfit was a problem beyond me, yet, without any consideration, doubt or even a halt, I passed across the end of the street to the rear of the farther row of cabins, and down the back of that row until I reached the nearest corner of the next to the last house. Here I halted and stood still. Why, I do not know, but I did, and it was my first halt since I had left my companions. Shortly after I halted I heard a voice that I recognized say:

"Lay over dar, you Taylor!"

Here I was, right where I wished to be, and in a very short time I had aroused the sleeping Garkeys, to learn that they had lain down to rest until the time appointed for the meeting, naturally falling fast asleep. They reproached themselves for their neglect, and we were soon on our way to the river bank, with a plentiful supply of food.

They asked me how I had found them, and I truthfully replied that I did not know, at which they rolled their eyes and looked at me in a peculiar manner, when I added that I was walking around the cabins in the hope of finding someone awake, and heard Sam tell Taylor to roll over. This satisfied them, but it has never satisfied me, for, while I heard the voice almost as soon as I halted, I could have passed the cabin in the short interval had I kept on, and in such event I could not have heard what I did.

My going directly to the cabins may be attributed to the instinct which sometimes leads men, and my passing to the rear of the farther cabins first to an accident of direction, but I never could account, on any theory of chance or instinct, for the coincidence of my halt at the proper place at the only instant in which I could have heard the call of Sam to Taylor.

We reached Rummel and Miller in so short a time after my departure from them as to cause an inquiry from them as to how I had managed to find the darkeys so quickly. I postponed explanation until later, and we proceeded to business.

The negroes had cooked us a goodly amount

of hog meat and a pone of corn bread, but the meat was only such as they could procure in a hurry, and consisted of the livers, lights, noses and such portions of the animal as would not be used by the planter and his family.

The skiff of the darkeys had been lodged, during high water, behind a tree, and when we got it down and afloat it looked like a sieve. We caulked it as best we could with leaves and some old rags, but the thing was a failure, and none of us cared to risk it.

Sam offered to pilot us to Little Rock himself, crossing the river lower down and then going across the country, but this offer we declined, because of the almost certainty of death if runaway prisoners were caught with a runaway negro. Sam still insisted, however, saying that he had a rifle and seven rounds of ammunition, and that we could fight if we had to, but we positively refused to take him with us, and the man was actually inclined to be angry. The matter was settled by Taylor giving us directions to follow the river down stream until we found a cabin in a certain spot, which he described, and we set off in high glee, Taylor further informing us that his name would make everything right with the owners of the cabin, and that we would find a willing and able ferryman there.

It was now nearly morning, and we hastened on our way; but, when we came to the spot where Taylor had told us we would find a path to the cabin, we found that a large force of cavalry had recently been camped there, and all signs of any regular path were completely obliterated by the trampled condition of the ground and the many trails leading in all directions, while an immense quantity of corn shucks were strewn all about the place.

We made a circuit of the camp, and finally struck off on a path which looked as if it might be the one meant by Taylor, but we had not gone a great ways when it became a blind lead, and we were soon lost in the canebrake. The cane made it too dark to proceed farther, and we went into camp.

When daylight came we found ourselves in a great bend of the river, and a little feeling around showed us a number of cavalry horses turned loose. We therefore kept quiet, in a part of the bottom where the cane was so thick that we once heard a man rounding up the horses without our being able to see him. As Rummel expressed it, "We couldn't have found a cow right there if we had had hold of her tail."

After a while we stole out to where we could see without being seen, and discovered a tent and big fire not far away, while in the distance was a band of music moving away with an escort of rebel cavalry. Around the tent and fire were a lot of men and cavalry horses, and we concluded to adjourn.

After a long search through the cane we found a road and started off, keeping a sharp lookout.

We had gone but a short distance down the road when we almost ran into another cavalry camp, and we had to swallow our hearts to keep them in their proper position, while we hastily executed a flank movement to avoid the soldiers. We succeeded in passing around them without being discovered, and again went on our way in peace for a time, but soon had another scare.

It was now nearly evening, and as we reached the river bank we heard some men approaching. It was a close shave, as we barely had time to conceal ourselves before they came out of the woods on the opposite side of the road and started for the camp we had just passed.

As soon as they had disappeared we started to follow the river bank, and as we proceeded down stream, with the timber on our right and the river on our left, we had not gone far when some men were heard coming in our direction. Dodging into the brush for concealment, we lay there until several men and their dogs had passed. They turned into the wood not far from us and began cutting down a tree in which they had located a coon. The tree was soon felled, and then occurred a lively skirmish between men, dogs, clubs and coon, in which the coon finally got the worst of it.

When the battle was over and the coon-hunters had gone, we crawled out of our hiding place and started down the river again.

In less than a mile, and about 12 o'clock, we came upon another lot of soldiers, camped in the road on the river bank and apparently sound asleep, our evidence of the latter fact being the unmusical sounds proceeding from them.

The situation was rather on the critical order, but it was light enough for us to see any movement of the enemy. We made a careful movement by the right flank, and were soon around them, fortunately without discovery.

Proceeding on our way, we would have felt quite happy had Miller been less miserable, but he could not forget that we had not as yet crossed the river, and it was impossible for him to be comfortable while on the wrong side of a stream of water.

Coming to an opening in the timber on our right we saw a plantation. A high fence was built along the road in front of it. Just as we had gotten fairly started away from the timber and in front of this fence the sounds of a horse galloping in our direction caused us to make a sudden choice between an unwise meeting and a slide down the steep river bank. We slid.

The horsemen reined up in front of the farm-house, just abreast of where we were hugging the slippery bank, and we heard him call out some inmate of the house and ask the way to

Rondo, where, it seemed, they were having a dance.

The danger to result from meeting with undesirable people was considerable, and we had quite a scare on account of our narrow margin of time for evading this fast rider, but we soon became glad of the forced tumble over the river bank.

As soon as we were recovered from our scare and momentary confusion we found that our slide down the bank had landed us within easy reach of a canoe, the very thing most needed by us at that time. In fact, if we had gone down the bank with more momentum either the canoe or the water under it would have stopped our descent.

This discovery seemed providential, and we regarded it as a good omen of our success.

An investigation proved the canoe to be a poor affair, but we concluded that we could cross two at a time, and Rummel and Miller started, I keeping pace with them on the bank as the canoe carried them down. They got over all right, and Miller landed, Rummel coming back for me. Both Miller and myself now walked down stream, as the canoe made as much distance that way as across, and when Rummel had finally picked me up and landed me we met Miller at least a mile down stream from where we had started the movement.

During this operation Miller and I had to keep

close to the river in order that we might not lose sight of each other or the canoe, and, by thus being unable to choose the best places for a convenient walk, we were pretty well scratched by the briers and other impediments that seemed to exist in profusion just where we had to go.

Having no further use for the canoe, we upset it and let it go. Then we started across the river bottom.

We had no trouble until we struck a bayou, which the moonlight showed to be quite wide. We could not tell how deep it was, but we found that it had a soft bottom, and we did not venture to wade the sluggish stream. After a long search up and down the edge, during which we got tangled up in some brush and made a row which started up some dogs in the neighborhood, we found a fence which crossed the bayou. I shall never forget the sight of Miller and Rummel "cooning" that fence.

The moon shone down through the gathering clouds with a dim light, and when we reached the fence we could see that it was built clear across the water in our front; so I mounted it at once and was soon on the other side. My companions had a discussion as to who should go first, both hanging back, for the fence looked frail and the top rails were sharp. When I got over and turned around to look, Rummel was just making a start.

The fence had not been used as a bridge, and

some of the rails were rotten, while most were slippery.

I had had some vexatious experiences myself in crossing, and I was in a position to enjoy keenly the sight of the others going through the same experiences; so I stood in the moonlight, encouraging my friends and laughing heartily as a slip on a broken rail caused suppressed comments or grotesque contortions on the part of the fence-riders. They finally got across, and we soon found the main road, but our troubles were not yet ended, for the soil was "gumbo" of the meanest kind, and we soon had to camp and rest up, while to add to our cheer and comfort it began to rain.

We spent the balance of the night in the rain and "gumbo," praying for daylight and sunshine.

CHAPTER XVIII.

EXPERIENCES.

The next morning we started on our way and had a routine march for several days, with no incidents worth mentioning until we began to meet a stray soldier now and then. Our growing confidence in ourselves made it easy for us to tell a satisfactory story in each case, and we learned from these men that we were approaching Washington, where Magruder had his headquarters.

From some negroes we got a full description of the town and a complete line of directions as to what course to pursue in order to avoid undesirable observation.

We had to be very careful, but boldness was an essential part of the policy of being careful, and we walked through the outskirts of the town as if we owned it, avoiding the traveled streets, but being as free and as easy as possible.

It was impossible for Miller to be free and easy at any time in anything partaking of deception, as he was too conscious and conscientious. No amount of successful evasion of difficulties could make him forget for a moment that we were escaped prisoners and should be locked up—from the standpoint of the rebels; so he was continually imagining that he saw detection in the eye of every person we met.

We were all nervous, but, with the exception of Miller, we made a fair show of being self-possessed and independent. We walked through the town as if traveling on eggs; every sound made him start; every person we saw gave him a shock of dread and uncertainty, and if we had met anyone of a suspicious nature we should have been closely questioned, at least. As it was, we finally skirted the town and got into the main road again, beyond, but we had to pass right through the soldiers' quarters to do it. We went on the principle that they were ignorant as to us, and would have no suspicions unless we created them by our actions, but only good luck in not being observed closely saved us from capture, for poor Miller scarcely touched the ground, and showed his effort at restraint so plainly that anyone with half an eye would have known that he was doing something wrong. We "herded" him between us as best we could, and, not being critically surveyed, succeeded in passing on our way.

The next night we came to a blacksmith shop, where we had to take refuge on account of a heavy rain. This shop was one of those old-fashioned country forges, built by the roadside near some farmer's house, where he or his neighbors tried their hands at smith work as occasion demanded. The building was an old "shack," with a leaky roof, but it gave some shelter, although we had to sleep on the forge as best we could, to keep out of the puddles and mud on the earthen floor.

I know of no word better than *excruciating*, to describe the comforts of that night. The forge was large, and we could lie upon it after cleaning it off, but we had to squeeze together. The edges were rough stones, and our feet hung over. If my readers will take the first opportunity afforded them to occupy a similar position for several hours they will appreciate my use of the above word. To enjoy fully the situation, aside from the pains thereof, they should have a friend stand by with some cold water and occasionally let fall a drop, or succession of them, upon the face, neck or ears of the victim. As a choice of two evils it was an admirable selection; as a matter of comfort it was a failure.

We were not awakened by the daylight, for we were already awake, and, when we could see that the rain had turned to snow, we started off again, preferring the snow and mud in daylight. Coming to an open piece of woods, and seeing a large tree which had been felled, we went to it and found what protection we could in its thick top for the balance of the day, the monotony of the stay being relieved by exchange from snow to rain and from rain to snow every now and then.

Just before dark it cleared up, and we once more started on our way, meeting with no obstacle until we reached the Little Missouri River bottom, which was crossed by an old corduroy road, and then we had some more fun.

For two miles and a half we blundered along on this road, in a gloomy darkness, every few minutes coming to a spot where one or the other of us would slip through between the logs and sink up to our knees in the mud and water, which fact was generally communicated to the others by harsh criticisms upon the efficiency of the county commissioners.

When we reached the river we were about as tired as men can be and stand up, but we found that the ferry-boat was on the other side, and we had to seek some place in which to rest for the night and await daylight. Going back a short distance from the river we found an open space where there were signs of a former camp, and we tried to build a fire. Everything was soaking wet, and all our efforts ended in smoke, except a few sulphurous remarks. There was no shelter to be had; we had to sleep in the open, and the ground was too wet to be comfortable. After some discussion, we decided to try standing up, which means of rest we enjoyed for the balance of the night.

Did you ever try to find a place to rest when everything upon which you could possibly sit or lie was soaking wet? If so, you can understand why we chose to stand up. Did you ever try to sleep in a standing posture, or to rest in like position for any length of time? If so, you will appreciate the following:

Throwing my blanket over my head, I braced myself firmly against a tree, closed my eyes, and—the next thing I knew I was in a heap on the wet ground, wildly struggling with my blanket, my knees having relaxed as I became unconscious. Now fully awake, I took a walk around to find a better spot, but soon came back to my first location and tried it again. This time I remained awake long enough to realize, by the time that the comfortable feelings of drowsiness were again stealing over me, that the air inside of my blanket was not pleasant to breathe, and, in throwing the covering from my head, I became wide awake again. After another interval of wakefulness, during which I realized keenly how tired my limbs were, and after quietly enjoying some of the experiences of my neighbors, the demands of nature again became paramount, and I dozed off. With a sudden sense of a harsh scraping along the back of my head, and a dim realization of the fact that my knees had again refused duty, I came to myself just in time to keep from sitting on the ground, this time sliding down the tree instead of pitching forward. After a walk down to the river to view the situation again, I returned to my tree, adjusted my position, to guard as well as I could against former experiences, and gradually dozed off in the belief that I was this time scientifically and safely propped. Suddenly I realized that I was falling, and became conscious enough to make three or four rapid steps forward, to save myself, before I stumbled over a log and went head first to the ground. After this, I never went to sleep during the balance of the night, but I contented myself with a succession of nods between the intervals of knee-bendings and losses of balance. Try it and see how it works.

I have slept on the wet ground—slept soundly, and never taken cold from it, but not in a boggy location such as that was on that night, and we all stood up in preference, again a choice of the lesser evil.

It might be asked why we did not go back to the high ground instead of remaining in the bottom. No one who has ever tramped over such a miserable road as that by which we had reached the bottom—for two and a half miles in the dark—will be likely to question why we preferred to stay where we were. It is doubtful whether we would have undertaken to retrace our steps over the corduroy road even if we had known in advance just what our night's experience was to be.

The next morning when we went down to the river we found that it had risen several feet during the night.

The road reached the river at a point of land which projected some distance, and where the road had been comparatively dry the night before, behind the point, we now had to wade in order to reach the ferry landing.

It was useless to attempt hailing the ferryboat, so we went back to our stamping ground and breakfasted upon what corn we could pick out of the ground around the spot where former campers had tarried. This corn was the scaled or wasted kernels left by horses at their feeding places.

While eating we heard a noise of men talking on the river, and at once assumed that the boat was coming over. We had no money with which to pay for crossing, and my companions, Miller especially, were very much excited over the question of what we were to do. Miller had a ring which he wanted me to take for the purpose of paying the ferryman, but I would not take it, and we nearly had a quarrel in consequence. My desire was to go to the ferry and be governed by circumstances as to what we should do, but the others wanted to have it all mapped out beforehand.

"What will you tell him, Swiggett?" asked Miller.

"How can I tell?" was my reply.

"But suppose he asks for money or is suspicious?"

"When he does or is I will meet him; but, boys, how on earth can you tell what to do or say till you know what you have to overcome? Let's go down there in a natural way and do what seems best when we get there. Come on!"

We went, my companions following me reluctantly, and Miller all in a flutter of nervous apprehension.

Reaching the landing, we found the boat nearly across, but the ferryman had all he could do to make any progress. The rise in the river had made a strong current along our shore. It was a hand ferry, and the rope was fastened in a poor line for ease in ferrying at that stage of the river.

Calling out to the man, I got in a good position to jump aboard, and said to my companions:

"Come on, boys! Can't you see that the man has his hands full? Let's jump aboard and help."

Hearing this, the fellow increased his efforts, the boat approached nearer, we made a big jump and got aboard, helping to haul the boat to the land. Then we learned that he had come over to shift the rope, and we helped him do this, after which he took us across.

Arriving on the other side I put my hand in my pocket as confidently as if I had had a roll of greenbacks at my command, and asked the ferryman how much we owed him. As I expected, he would not take a cent, but thanked us heartily for our assistance, and we went on our way rejoicing.

It is a fact worthy of note that the response of this man to my offer of pay was almost as well known to me before he made it as after. Not on the principle of natural results from given causes, as many men would have asked either all or part pay. Nor was it from any particular judgment of the individual, as I was unable to form any satisfactory idea of his inclination from what could be seen of him. I simply *felt* and *knew* that he would refuse pay. Whether this was due to intuition, instinct or some subtle principle of mind communication, I do not profess to know and I do not say, but the fact was that I did not think or believe—I *knew*, and those inclined to account for the fact will find this point of interest to them.

"What would you have said, Swiggett, if he had named a price?" asked Miller.

"But he didn't, Miller," I responded; "and he wasn't suspicious."

"But if he had been?"

"How can I tell? It would have depended on circumstances. My experience is that one can never, or very seldom, carry out imaginary conversation, and I never try to hamper myself unnecessarily by pre-arranged ideas."

These conversations are related simply to show how easy it is to overcome many seeming

CAPT. B. F. MILLER.

difficulties. We can figure and calculate all we will in advance, but it almost invariably happens that the details of our plans must be changed on the scene of action, either to surmount unexpected obstacles or to take the shortest and surest road to success. The best way to dispose of obstacles is to go at them. Many and most disappear before you reach them, while those which really have to be surmounted are usually ridden over on lines suggested at the time of meeting.

In crossing the river we had given the ferryman no time to ask questions, even had he been disposed to do so, and I had asked the way to Arkadelphia, learning the direction to take and that the distance was fifty-two miles, on a plain road.

As usual, after the river was crossed, Miller was jubilant and happy until he had time to begin worrying about the next river, which he soon did. If my friend worries as much about crossing the final river as he did about crossing earthly rivers in our travels together it may be that he will have to cross much sooner than he otherwise would.

It must not be understood that my illustrations of Miller's peculiarities are made in disparagement of the man. We all have our own peculiar traits of character, and it merely happened that this journey developed in Miller some phases of a disposition that in other things would have had more than compensating merits. He was simply more cautious than is usual in men, and so exceedingly honest that it was impossible for him to dissimulate. A tall, fine-looking gentleman, with dignified bearing, and the very embodiment of honor and conscientiousness, one to whom recapture was certain if lies were necessary to avoid it; this was Miller.

CHAPTER XIX.

GOOD LUCK AND BAD.

We were soon out of the river bottom, and then came the question as to whether we should keep or avoid the road. We decided to remain upon it, because of the fact that the ferryman would probably ask the first comer if he had met us, and a negative reply might cause questions and suspicions; so we trudged along, in hopes of a successful issue to our campaign.

Soon we saw an approaching horseman, and again our friend Miller became agitated. When a nearer view developed the fact that the rider was a rebel officer, we had hard work to keep Miller from throwing up his hands or running, we being entirely unarmed, but he calmed down and behaved nicely as the officer rode up and we saw that he was a major.

We saluted, said good morning, and passed on in a matter-of-fact way, while the officer gave us scarcely a look as he returned our salute and rode by; so Miller had a respite.

Having thus met somebody to report us at the ferry, we now left the road and went into the woods to lay up, taking pains to go a good mile from the road in order to avoid any possible notice.

Finding a good, thick top of a felled tree, we sought the seclusion of its branches and indulged in a good sleep.

We were awakened along in the afternoon by a crunching sound like that of horses walking on gravel, and, when we realized what it was, the horses were so close to us that we fairly hugged the ground and trembled, feeling that it must be some people looking for us.

The sound passing by, we got out to investigate, and we had not gone fifteen paces through some bushes till we stopped and looked at each other quizzically. There was another road, evidently more traveled than the one we had taken such pains to avoid. As the joke was on all, we had nothing to say.

We were now out of provisions again, and, in prospecting around, we found that the two roads came together a short distance below.

The country in our neighborhood was a farming district, but it was now barren. The houses and buildings were deserted, the fences down and everything dilapidated. We could find nothing to eat, and again took to the road.

To show how run down and deserted that section was I state as a fact that we ransacked every stable, corn crib and vacant house in our path that night for a distance of about fifteen miles without seeing a soul or finding anything eatable. But few houses appeared to be inhabited, and these were avoided.

Just before daybreak we came across an old stable, where we found some corn in the mangers—that is, the small kernels left on the ends of the cobs by horses when they eat. Of this we made a fairly good meal.

A little farther on we came to a corn crib which had in it about 150 bushels of corn, and here we had a feast, building a fire and parching the corn.

While we were eating we saw a cow coming toward the corn crib, and we welcomed her heartily, giving her some corn shucks to feed upon while we milked her and regaled ourselves.

We now proceeded with little or no trouble, making far better time than we had expected to make, and we felt almost as if at home when we came to a finger-board bearing the inscription: "2½ miles to Arkadelphia."

I had been in this place with our army on our way to Camden the spring before, and it now seemed as if we must soon meet some blue uniforms.

We passed on around the town to the Caddo river, which empties into the Washita four miles above Arkadelphia.

When we reached the river there were no signs of a ferry, and we walked up and down the river bank for about two miles each way before we found any chance to cross. There seemed to be no ferry, and the chance of crossing was based solely upon the fact that we finally discovered a house on the farther bank, and a skiff tied to a tree near by.

We built our hopes on that skiff, but there was no way to get it at present, and we decided to drop down the river to a secluded place in the bottom and await developments.

Finding the desired place, we went into camp, building a fire, parching some corn, warming up well and getting a good sleep.

In the morning we again went over the ground, but found no better chance to cross, concluding that the owner of the skiff must be the ferryman.

We could not build a raft, as there were no logs lying about which were suitable for the purpose. The river was too deep to wade, and the water was so cold that we were afraid to risk an effort to swim over, especially on account of Miller's aversion to the element, and the necessity of towing him over on a log if we tried this method of crossing; so, after sizing up the situation in all its aspects, we decided to keep quiet until about sundown and then go boldly down to the water's edge at the road and hail the ferryman, taking our chances of results.

Accordingly we again sought our hiding place, and passed the day in sleeping and conversation, neither hearing nor seeing anything throughout the day.

At the proper time we emerged boldly from our secluded nook and sought the road, without any attempt at secrecy, having been all over the ground both in the morning and the night before, and having heard nothing since.

A short distance from the road we saw a man on the river bank, and kept right on, taking him to be some stray individual looking for a chance to cross the river, but we had not gone twenty paces after seeing him until we walked right into a picket post of nine men, or, rather, right into plain view of them, they being about fifty yards distant.

There was no help for it but to put on a bold front, and we walked right along about our business. Seeing them watching us, I broke the silence by addressing them and asking the way to the ferry.

They answered, and asked where we were going, to which I responded by saying that we had been hunting for the ferry for an hour or more and were going to cross, walking along in a business-like manner while talking.

The corporal in charge of the picket guard now called to us to come into camp, but we did not hear him, and kept on without hurrying. Then we got a peremptory order in a tone which meant business, and we concluded instantaneously to hear and heed this; so we stopped and asked what they wanted, and walked slowly into camp when the corporal repeated his order, remonstrating against the delay as we did so.

Miller was now so nervous that he scarcely knew on which end he stood, but he quieted down in appearance when I asked him to keep cool, let me do the talking, and back me up.

We were now asked to show our papers, but we had none to show, and by rapid questioning I learned that these men had been guarding the river at this point for some time, but had left the river bank for better quarters when the high water came, and had just camped again when we came up.

Asking the corporal his name, I learned that it was Ed. Rocket, and I then told him that we lived in Rockport, Hot Springs county, and were going home, being soldiers in Captain Stewart's Company A, of the 15th Arkansas, and having come from Magruder's headquarters at Washington.

He then asked for our passes, and I told him that he was too old a soldier not to know that we could not possibly have a pass, it being all that a captain's commission was worth to give leave of absence in those days, stating to him, in explanation of our absence from our command, that we had been in service for over two years without any leave; that when we had begged our captain to let us go home when it was so close he had told us that we could simply slip off, if we would promise to be back in ten days, and he would not report us absent unless that time elapsed before our return, and that we had taken chances on his word, because we wanted to get home so badly.

This seemed to satisfy Rocket that it was all right, and he hesitated for a few minutes before he answered that he would gladly let us go on, but that his orders were positive to let *nobody* cross the river without a pass or proper papers.

I again remonstrated at the delay and annoyance, and he sympathized with us, but was firm in his unwillingness to disobey positive orders which left no discretion. He finally said he would take us over to headquarters at Arkadelphia and do what he could to get necessary permission for us to cross the river.

There being no other course to pursue, we thanked him heartily and at once fraternized with him and his men.

They had just cooked supper, and we invited ourselves to eat with them, saying that we were almighty hungry, but that they would have to put up with it, inasmuch as we were not exactly willing guests.

We were quite hungry, and we demonstrated the fact by eating the entire quantity of food which the nine men had prepared for their meal, talking and chatting the while, with the party looking on with open-mouthed amazement at our appetites, as they waited for two of their number to prepare an additional supply, the extra quantity being increased as they proceeded, until they really cooked as much more as they had at first prepared for themselves.

Once, while we were eating, Miller inadvertently called me captain, and asked me to pass him something. Fortunately he did not speak loud, as he was close by my side, but I gave him a look which spoke volumes, and he kept silent thereafter.

After our hosts had finished their supper we started for Arkadelphia, and, while on the road, we learned that the object of guarding the river had been to catch refugee "Arkansaw" people and to head off such natives as might be en route to join the 3d and 4th Arkansas Cavalry, then being organized in Little Rock.

This was our twenty-first night out since leaving the stockade, and we were now 275 miles from Tyler, Texas, and fifty miles from Little Rock—"so near and yet so far."

CHAPTER XX.
IN THE TOILS.

On reaching Arkadelphia we were taken to the provost marshal's office, which was located in a two-room house in the centre of the town, and there we found a lieutenant at the desk in one of the rooms, while fourteen or fifteen men were gathered around an old-fashioned fireplace, telling stories and spending a pleasant evening. Some of these men were soldiers and some were not.

I shall never forget that little room in that old house. It was about twelve feet by sixteen, the walls were bare, the ceiling was low and smoke-stained, the floor was without covering, and the only furniture was the old table which served as a desk for the lieutenant, a number of more or less rickety chairs and the two huge old-fashioned andirons which supported the blazing logs in the enormous, ancient fireplace.

Rocket took the lieutenant aside and told him our story, the evident impression being that it was all right. He then left us.

They had a lot of cooking utensils, bedding, etc., in the second room, and soldiers were passing in and out of the rooms at intervals.

As we stood awaiting the termination of the interview between Rocket and the lieutenant, I thought I recognized several of the men in the room, and I was certain as to two of them. It is needless to say that I avoided observation as much as possible, without seeming to do so, and I was not recognized.

As Rocket left, the lieutenant came up to us, and, evidently thinking it necessary, as a matter of form, began asking questions.

I told the same story that I had told to Rocket, while Miller and Rummel got into the crowd before the fireplace, adding that we were from Northern Missouri in the first place, that my wife was the sister of my two companions, that their name was Miller and mine Swiggett, and that we had had to leave Missouri when it had gotten hot up there, coming to "Arkansaw" and joining the 15th "Arkansaw."

While telling this story, which I did in response to questions asked, I could hear comments on the side between the men sitting around, and heard one say that Rockport was not in Hot Springs county, and then another say that it was and that I was right.

These comments disturbed Miller so much that he could not keep quiet to save his soul, and I nearly laughed out aloud as I got a side look at him and saw him shifting nervously from one foot to the other, now rubbing his hands together spasmodically, and then recollecting himself enough to hold them out to the fire as an excuse for the rubbing, every second or two casting a "sheep's glance" over his shoulder at the lieutenant and myself.

His actions evidently excited suspicions, for, just as I was certain that the lieutenant was satisfied, and felt confident that all was well, he asked me whom I knew up around Rockport, and then commenced going back over the same ground again in a cross-questioning sort of way.

I told him that I knew no one up that way except our own folks, and, as I heard a side comment of "Damned strange," I turned on the speaker and said emphatically:

"No, it isn't 'damned strange,' if you will let me tell my own story, and not try to put words in my mouth."

"Well, go on," said one fellow, and I continued:

"When we left Missouri and joined the regiment we left our families behind in Northern Missouri. They were ostracized and misused because we had gone off and joined the rebels, and life became a burden to them. So, when Price made his last raid into Missouri, they were only too glad to come with him and take chances of starving among friends in preference to accepting the grudging charity of the Yankees. They were compelled to stop in Hot Springs county, five miles southeast of Rockport. We have never been in Hot Springs county ourselves, and have not seen our families since we left them in Northern Missouri."

The lieutenant now asked me if I had no papers at all.

Quick as a flash I said "Yes," and produced from my pocket a newspaper published in Washington the day before, which I had picked up on the road as we came in.

He looked at it, laughed, and said that he did not mean that sort of paper, but a pass or something to prove our identity.

I said that we would not be there if we had any pass, and that I did not see why he doubted a straight statement in accordance with facts.

He now led me into the next room and tried to coax me into confidence with him, but I stuck to my text, and could see that I had him on the run, so to speak, although he had apparently suspected us of being Arkansas Federals.

As we walked back to the office room I saw that poor Miller was as fidgety as a nervous man could possibly be, and his actions, as he quickly held out his hands to the fire and as quickly withdrew them to rub them together in an absent-minded way, caused the lieutenant to look at me sharply and again ask to what regiment we belonged.

This made me mad, and I answered shortly:

"The 15th Arkansaw, as I have told you three times before."

"What brigade?" now followed quickly.

"Thompson's," was the prompt reply.

"What division?"

"Molyneux's."

At this time we had been under fire for nearly an hour and a half without giving anything tangible on which the lieutenant could hang suspicion, but here he thought he had me, and he quickly responded:

"There are no Arkansaw troops in Molyneux's division."

Without an instant's hesitation, I came back at him with:

"If you know more about this thing than I do, perhaps you had better tell the story. I'm in the 15th Arkansaw, and Molyneux is our division commander."

The principle upon which I went in this examination was that these men were most likely as ignorant as myself about matters not of general importance, and I knew that they could only go on hearsay as to minor matters, such as what troops made up a division at a certain time when that division was widely scattered, and I therefore stood on my dignity and was positive.

My reply plainly staggered the lieutenant, and he fell back on what was apparently his last ground of argument, as he looked at our dress and asked how we came by our blue blouses and breeches.

I laughed carelessly, and looked over the crowd in a quizzical way as I answered:

"If you fellows had been chasing Steele's

army all summer as we have you would be wearing them too."

Then, turning to the lieutenant again, I said:

"Now, see here, Lieutenant, you know that there is no such thing as a leave of absence to be had in our army nowadays; we wouldn't have any army if there was; and when men have been in hard service for over two years without a chance to see their folks, it's blamed tough to keep them standing around answering fool questions when they have only ten days in which to go home and get back."

I saw in the lieutenant's face that our case was won, but, as he opened his mouth to say the words which would set us free, I heard the question from behind:

"Where was your regiment raised?"

Turning, I saw that it had proceeded from a bright-looking young fellow of about sixteen or seventeen, who sat near Miller and was looking up at him with a quizzled glance. My heart sank within me, but I answered promptly:

"In Clar—"

"Hold on, there! I didn't ask you," interrupted the young fellow; "I haven't a bit of doubt but that you can tell every township that furnished a man, and probably name every man in the regiment if necessary; but you have had to do a lot of talking for your crowd, and I would like to hear this man answer the question."

I now knew that we were caught, and I almost

laughed, even in my misery, at the picture before me.

Miller was almost paralyzed. He hemmed and hawed an instant and looked inquiringly at the lieutenant and myself.

"Answer the question," sharply said that worthy, as he at once caught the drift of the young fellow's remarks and had all his old suspicions awakened again by the pitiful uncertainty of Miller's actions.

"In—In—In Clar—Hem! In Clar—Hem! Hem!—H-e-m! Really, gentlemen—" he said, as he rubbed his hands and made all sorts of faces and turned all colors, while vainly trying to recall some names that he might safely use.

He finally stammered out:

"The adjoining counties to—to—in the northern part of the State."

His questioner then remarked quizzically:

"Well, I'll be ——, if here ain't a fellow that has been in the army over three years and can't name the counties in which his regiment was raised."

"Take these men to the jail," now ordered the lieutenant, and we were led off to that place of abode, hearing, as we left the room, various interesting comments and much laughter.

They put us in a cabin, which was lined throughout with sheet iron, and which had no opening in it except the door. A pine torch furnished the light. The floor was covered with filth, and we had not been in there five minutes before the atmosphere had become almost unbearable.

I kicked loudly against the door, and soon a sergeant came to know what was wanted. He was told that we wanted to see the lieutenant at once, and he went away to call him.

When the officer came he was followed by a curious crowd, and, as they opened the door, I stepped forward and asked pleasantly if that was the way to treat Federal prisoners.

The lieutenant said that we were held as suspicious parties who could not account for themselves, and who were probably endeavoring to join the Yankee regiments now being organized in Little Rock, but that if we could satisfy him that we were Federal prisoners he would let us out and treat us as such.

Having made up our minds that our best course now was to be frank, we told him who we really were, and that we had escaped from the stockade at Tyler, Texas, and made our way so far north on foot.

As I told this I heard a remark in the crowd:

"Damned if they didn't deserve to get through."

The lieutenant turned, with a frown, and asked who made the remark, but he had a smothered grin on his face as he turned back and invited us out.

This remark seemed to be the sentiment of the

entire outfit, although they now had to keep us, and intended to do so.

We were taken to a room in a neighboring house and a guard was placed over us, but we held a regular levee until far into the night, the whole town apparently coming to see and talk with us.

While we were chagrined and disappointed over our capture, we yet had enough sense to make the best of it, and I cannot remember a night when I had any more fun than that levee afforded.

The crowd ridiculed the lieutenant, praised the young fellow who had shown us up, mimicked poor Miller until he was nearly frantic, laughed and joked with us, asked us innumerable questions about ourselves, and generally made us feel more like being out for a lark than in confinement as prisoners.

During the evening we told them of our hard fare while en route, and described our appropriation of the picket post's supper, at which they all laughed. Then we suggested that we were even then quite hungry, and asked for something to eat.

After some delay they brought us a kettle of cooked fresh pork and some meal for a pone of bread. There was probably about four pounds of pork in the mess, and a goodly supply of bread, but we ate it all before bedtime, holding our informal reception meanwhile.

CHAPTER XXI.

ANOTHER RETURN TRIP.

We remained at Arkadelphia for several days before we were moved to Magruder's headquarters at Washington, and during this wait we were treated more like guests than prisoners, excepting, of course, the being under guard. I do not think that there was an able-bodied personage in the place who did not come to see us, and there were several callers who were not able-bodied.

All the people were curious to see us, because we were Yankees, and more curious because of our successful escape to this point, while our almost successful effort to get through at the last was the occasion of much admiration, many jokes and friendly actions.

When we did not give ourselves time to think of our capture we really enjoyed our stay.

In due course of time the guards who had captured us were detailed to take us back, and they were given a leave of twenty days in which to do so, Rocket now being a sergeant.

Our start was made after a farewell that showed far more friendship than enmity, and we made the fifty miles to Washington in four days, taking it easy.

Of the nine men who composed this squad eight were positively disloyal to the Confederacy, but were forced to fight for it because of their homes and families.

Each one of the eight, at different times, talked very freely to me when the others were not around, and each one told me that they would never have held us at the river if the others could have been certainly depended upon not to report the matter. We got to be very friendly with these guards, and we were really sorry when it came time to part from them.

One of our guards was an old man whom his companions called Captain Payne. He rode a sorry-looking specimen of a horse and was evidently only a private. Wishing to be friendly, he offered to let me ride his horse if I would allow him to hold the halter, which offer I promptly accepted, informing him that he was welcome to hold the halter and the horse's tail as well if he so desired. As an apology for the limitation of my actions with his horse, he informed me that he had positive orders to let us have no chance of escape, and to shoot us without notice if such an attempt was made.

In the course of conversation I asked him why he was called captain while being under orders of a sergeant. His reply was that he had been elected captain of 500 men who had organized to resist the draft and afterwards joined the Federal army; that they had been informed upon and the scheme frustrated, he having been forced to compromise between his neck and the halter by enlisting in the Confederate army as a private.

We were taken up behind on the horses of our guards during part of the trip, and in one of these rides behind Sergeant Rocket I learned that he had been in Missouri with Price, but had disliked the job very much, as had most of his companions. When Price had commenced his retreat he had simply broken ranks and ordered the men to fall in again at Boggy Hollow. They had all been forced to shift for themselves, and for three days he had had nothing to eat. After that they had lived almost entirely on fresh meat, without salt, for twenty-four days, and the organization had been largely broken up.

Rocket told me that most of the people in his part of the country would hail with joy the approach of the Federal troops. He was married to the daughter of a planter, who was a Union man, though a slaveholder, and had joined the Confederate army to save his family. His father-in-law lived on the road ten miles north from Washington, and he described the location and gave directions so that I could find the house if I had another chance to run away, saying that if I ever reached there and made myself

SERGEANT E. B. ROCKET.

known I would certainly get to Little Rock in safety.

Captain Payne, also, gave me directions how to find the home of his people, telling me how to find Dooley's ferry, in the neighborhood, and how Dooley would know me, set me across the river and see that I reached the right place. He also told me that a neighbor of theirs had three sons in the Federal army at Little Rock, and that I could easily get horses and guides to that place.

When we reached Washington, and Ed. Rocket bade us good-bye, he told me that he had never been so sorry for anything in his life as that he had been obliged to capture and hold us.

Ed. Rocket is now a poor Baptist preacher in Arkansas.

We were turned into a guardhouse that was about sixty by twenty feet in size and so full that all could not lie down at once. It was far from being pleasant.

The prisoners confined in this building were three spies and a large number of Confederates, the latter being held for crimes ranging all the way from chicken-stealing to murder, and in this agreeable society we spent ten days.

We got acquainted with a good many of the prisoners, and had considerable fun in various ways, but we were glad to leave.

Cornmeal was the only food served to us during our stay, but the rebel prisoners were treated the same as the others, and we had an extra allowance as officers—by purchase; so we could not complain of any unfair distinctions.

There was one old skillet in the guardhouse, and all the cooking had to be done with this one article. It was never cool. We took turns in its use, and the call of "Next!" was as orderly and regular as in a barber shop.

By common consent the Yankees were given the first turn with this skillet, as preferred guests, and we thereby had our meals at ordinary meal hours.

There were crowds coming in and going out of the guardhouse all the time, as there was a regular system being carried out of securing cavalry horses for other sections.

In this part of the country they had more cavalry than infantry, while in other sections much of the veteran cavalry was dismounted for want of horses. So they would put these cavalrymen under arrest for chicken-stealing or any offense whenever possible and appropriate their horses for service elsewhere. Infantrymen were let off for the same offenses.

One of the rebel officers in charge offered to let us out if we would join his company, but we declined, with thanks.

There was plenty of money among the prisoners, and much poker-playing to kill time.

I had a toothpick, made of bone and representing a woman, for which I got fifty cents in silver.

With this amount I bribed one of the guards to get us four dozen eggs. Some of these we ate ourselves, but we sold the most of them to the prisoners for $1 apiece in Confederate money. These eggs were procured by the guard from some paroled Federal prisoners on the outside.

On the day following our egg deal I got permission to go outside with a guard for some water, and then secured permission to buy some supplies and take them inside. After some hunting around we found a nigger who had a lot of turnips, and I bought a bushel for $10 in Confederate money, having a good margin left. We ate all the turnips we wanted, and then got $1 apiece for the balance. Everything went at $1 a unit in Confederate money. Keeping this thing up, we fed ourselves well during our stay, and when we left we had $400 in Confederate money.

Two of the spies mentioned were named Honeycut and Masterson, and the latter was kept in irons. They had money, and secured extra food from the outside, of which we got a share.

Masterson had been captured with a lot of drugs in his possession, and he had claimed to be from Georgia, to which part of the country he was returning after having run the blockade with his drugs from the North, but he had forgotten to make all his stories agree, and they had arrested him as a spy and put leg-irons upon him. Later on, he joined the Confederate army to save his neck.

Honeycut claimed to have been a Copperhead in Ohio, and that he had been drafted and had furnished a substitute, but had then been drafted the second time, when he had sworn that he would not stand it. He claimed to have sent his family to Matamoras, and that he had gone to New York to join them by steamer, but had been unable to get a passport. He had then made his way to New Orleans, and had again failed to slip through. As a last resort he had gone to Arkansas and secured a pony, with the intention of riding through to Mexico, but had been captured and lost the horse and his money.

The provost marshal, Colonel Province, was a very clever gentleman, and he was kind to us in several ways. One of his courtesies was to grant us a parole within the city limits.

When Magruder's chief of staff saw us on the street and learned of our parole he ordered Colonel Province to return us immediately to prison. The colonel pleaded for us, saying that he knew us to be gentlemen, and that he felt easier in regard to us while we were on parole than he would if we were in the insecure guardhouse, even while he knew that the parole was contrary to orders, for the guardhouse was filthy and crowded with criminals. This plea in our favor had no effect, and the colonel received peremptory orders to place us in prison at once, under penalty of being reported to Magruder for disobedience.

Three guards were sent to take us to the colonel's headquarters, where he told us of his talk with the chief of staff, and expressed his regret that he was compelled to obey, closing his remark with:

"But I want to tell you, gentlemen, I am an original rebel from South Carolina, while that —— —— of a staff officer is from Chicago."

The colonel evidently thought that being a Northern man and a rebel would account for most any kind of meanness.

While defeated in his good intentions in the matter of parole, the colonel tried to make up for it in other ways. He gave me a pair of shoes which had been given to him by the Yankees while he had been a prisoner at Johnson's Island, and which I sold to Masterson for $250, for the purchaser could not wear his boots and leg-irons at the same time.

Our stay at Washington was prolonged on account of a lack of provisions to furnish the extra supply needed for a guard and ourselves on a journey. When it seemed certain that provisions were not to be forthcoming we were started off for Magnolia, Ark., which point we had to make without any supplies save what we could gather as we went along.

When we left Washington we stopped in front of the provost marshal's office, and Colonel Province came out to bid us good-bye and express his regrets that he had been prevented from according us the same kind treatment which he had received at Johnson's Island.

The first night out we reached Spring Hill, which was then a courier station, and were confined in an old church. One of the soldiers killed a hog, which proceeding was an outrageous violation of orders, as well as of the rights of the owner, but we had to eat. A guard and myself went to a neighboring house to get a kettle in which to cook the meat.

The difference between pork and beef in that country was about the same in those days as the difference between greenbacks and Confederate money.

The guard found a negro woman in the house, and he asked for something to eat. She gave us some beef and corn bread, but had no pork when asked for it. In the course of the conversation the guard told her who I was and about the escape of my companions and myself, when the darkey remembered that there was some cold pork in an outhouse, and produced it.

We got the necessary kettle and cooked our meat before we went on our way.

After we had again started, the guards paroled us, and several of them went home, appointing a meeting place and promising us more pork and some biscuit when they returned, which promise they kept.

When we reached Magnolia we found a camp of about forty badly wounded Federal prisoners there, who were the remnants of Steele's fight at Jenkins' Ferry.

We were put in jail for several days to await a move of this camp to Shreveport.

When all were ready the convalescent cases were loaded on wagons and we started.

CHAPTER XXII.

FORAGING, AND A NEW PRISON.

During this trip our rations were salt beef and corn bread, but the latter was unfit to eat, and I refused all rations, preferring to take the chances of foraging until we reached Shreveport.

On the first day out we made about twelve miles. At dusk it commenced to rain, and we camped in an old church at a cross roads. The wounded men and ourselves were placed in one end of the building, they on one side and we on the other, while the other end was used by our guards. They piled up all their equipments in one corner, and spread their blankets in the vacant space, then going off to a stillhouse in the neighborhood, where they got gloriously drunk, and leaving only a sentinel at the door.

When leaving Washington our party had been increased by three more runaways, who bore the names of Robinson, Fenton and Stanton, so that we were now six in all.

The guard at the door excited my envy, soon after his companions had left, by coolly drawing from his haversack a lot of biscuits and the ham of a shote. As he drew out his huge knife and began slicing off tempting bits of lean meat my envy overcame any timidity I may have had, and I determined to have some of that meat by fair means or foul.

Stanton came up to me as I came to this conclusion, and I remarked to him that I was about to take supper with the rebel. His curiosity spurred me on, and I walked out to the sentinel and asked if I could have some of his meat and biscuit. Much to my surprise and pleasure he promptly said: "Tub ber shure," and sliced off for me a liberal allowance of ham, giving it to me with some biscuits. My success led Stanton to follow suit, and we both had a fair meal with the generous fellow.

It was now getting dark, and the rain kept coming down. We had full possession of the room, and as Stanton and myself walked back to our companions, we saw Fenton eating. Inquiry developed the fact that he had been plundering the piled-up haversacks while we had been outside, and when we learned that there was a supply still unappropriated we promptly set out to empty the haversacks of everything desirable. During our talk together the sentinel had added his haversack to the pile, and the first thing to which we came was the balance of the ham from which we had just dined, together with fourteen biscuits. We felt awfully mean about it, but "self-preservation is the first law of nature," and we cleaned that bone, throwing it and the haversack behind the wainscoting.

This food was sufficient for our wants, and we would have been satisfied but that we found Rummel on one side eating some light bread, which he had purloined from another haversack. This made us ambitious again, so we went back and took all the desirable stuff we could find in the pile for future use.

We got a lot of light bread, about a pound and a half of butter and some sweet potatoes.

The wounded men had a kettle for cooking, and I borrowed this, built a fire in the stove and cooked our sweet potatoes.

About this time some of the guards came back, and one of them came to me to borrow the kettle, saying that he had some sweet potatoes to cook.

I told the man that he would have to wait until our stuff was cooked, and he sat down quietly and waited, chatting with us to pass away the time. When our potatoes were cooked we gave him the utensil, which he filled with water and put on the fire before he went for his potatoes. Then there was a row, as his potatoes happened to be those boiled by us.

Of course he could not identify the property, and I was indifferent, but to my surprise, instead of accusing us, he did not seem to suspect anyone save his comrades, and his accusation against them caused the rest to investigate on their own hook. The row that now ensued took a direction which we had not calculated upon, and we finally got well scared. The men were all more or less drunk, and their denunciations and reproaches of each other caused a row among themselves. The rest of the party came back, and there was more investigation, more row and much confusion. There were two classes of men in this crowd. About half were poor whites, of the ignorant, malicious sort, and the balance of a better class.

The question finally settled down to a denunciation of us by the first-named portion, and accusations against them by the others. At this stage of the game they began to talk of searching us, and we got scared, for we had too much on hand to be able to "bluff" them off in a general search, and their condition of excitement would not give us much chance for argument.

We now did what might seem to be a very mean thing, but it was done on the principle that, while our conviction of the robbery might, in their present state, mean death to us, they might curse and swear mightily, but would not harm anyone if they found the balance of their stuff where we put it—among the wounded men. We hid it around as best we could and awaited developments with much interest, but the row finally quieted down and we all went to sleep.

We were up very early in the morning, as we had to dispose of the plunder in some way, and went to work, for it was work. We ate all we possibly could, including the butter, and stuffed the remainder inside of our shirts. I had a butter taste in my mouth for a week afterward, and it was a good while before I could eat the article with my former relish.

Our guards made a partial search before we started, but they did not attempt to be too personal, and we evaded the discovery of any of the purloined food. It was plainly to be seen that we were now suspected, but they rather regarded the thing as a good joke, now that they were sober, and the search was for something to eat rather than to prove anything.

We now had several days of travel and similar scenes, but the robberies were now joint expeditions against the potato holes on the line of our road, where the surplus of the crop was stored for the winter, and the guards and ourselves shared alike in the guilt and proceeds.

When we reached Shreveport, we were taken through the town to Four Miles Springs, where I had been before, and here we were kept for six weeks.

A stockade and quarters had been built since my former visit, and things were much more comfortable.

We soon built a comfortable cabin in partnership with some other captured runaways who had just been brought to this stockade, and one of these, Lieutenant Bushnell, of the 120th

Illinois, became my berthmate when lots were cast to see who should occupy the several rude bunks erected in our mansion.

Sweet potatoes at this time were $10 a bushel in Confederate money, and my supply of cash came in so handy that we were enabled to refuse all rations and to live on the fat of the land; but we did not risk the gout by so doing. The fat of the land in those days was so well streaked with lean that everyone had to take much lean in order to get any fat, and the rebels themselves did not live in luxury.

There were about 250 prisoners now at this point. The rations served to them were brought in on a board. In order to get the privilege of doing our own cooking we asked and obtained special permission to have our rations served raw, and so we managed to have what we wanted.

There was a "greaser," from Mexico, on the outside, who made and sold potato pies. I would get five for a $5 bill and give Bushnell two. At the next pie meal he would reverse the order of things.

We made the acquaintance of a squad of men from the 16th Regiment of Indiana Mounted Infantry, their leading spirit being a Captain Moore.

At roll-call the guards made the prisoners stand out in line, and Moore was frequently prodded with a sword for hanging back and delaying matters.

One day we made an excellent dummy from an old log and some clothes, and carefully deposited it in Moore's bunk, covering it naturally with what bedclothes we had. At next roll-call Moore was not to be found, and the guards, after much swearing, went up to his cabin and found him, apparently, in bed and asleep. After several calls and shakes, accompanied by some artistic profanity, one of them prodded him gently with his sword. A little harder punch followed, when he still slept, and then a vicious one, when they threw back the covers and discovered the deception. A crowd had followed them, and they were now well laughed at, but they took it good-humoredly, only swearing at Moore for his deviltry. When we went back to roll-call Moore was in his place in line, and, as he gave a good excuse for absence and disclaimed all knowledge of any joke, the guards had to be satisfied with some general cussing.

The rebel prisoners were also kept in this stockade—men who, as at Washington, were imprisoned for various crimes and offenses.

One rebel prisoner complained of a theft. Moore hunted around, found a suspect, convened a court-martial, had the man tried, found guilty and sentenced to receive ten lashes, which were duly administered.

The court-martial and punishment are

worthy of note. All the preparations for the trial were made in due and ancient form, as formally as if it had been ordered by the regularly-constituted authorities in military life. The army (the prisoners) was well represented by a judge-advocate, and the culprit by "learned counsel." The offender was placed on the stand, and then witnesses for both sides were thoroughly questioned and cross-questioned. Being found guilty in usual form, the prisoner was sentenced as solemnly as if before a regular court. The punishment was given by causing the thief to be bent over a stump, with his hands and feet held by Confederate prisoners, while the ten stripes were laid on with a halter strap in the hands of another, who did not spare the victim. The rebel prisoners endorsed the proceedings as being perfectly legal and just.

The feverish desire to escape was constantly present with every man in the stockade, but there seemed to be little chance for getting away. We were allowed to go out after wood, but there was a guard for each prisoner when we went.

One rebel guard talked to me, and made a proposal. He was a rebel from principle, he said, but had lost everything, and was now over forty years old. What the outcome was to be he did not know, but he did know that he wanted to make some money for himself and family, and had a chance to do so if he had some help.

He told me of two steamboats, loaded with cotton, then lying tied up on Red River, not over five miles away, and kept in readiness for a run up some secluded bayou if the Yankees approached, calling my attention to the fact that, as only two guards protected each vessel, the fires kept in the furnaces made it a comparatively easy job to capture and get away with one of the boats and its load. He said that he had contemplated the capture of one boat for the purpose of taking it to New Orleans and selling the cotton, but had given up the idea of trying it as originally intended, fearing that the cotton and boat would be confiscated at New Orleans, because he was a rebel, even if he succeeded in getting there.

The suggested scheme struck me as being a good one, and in several trips made outside for wood with this man as my guard we perfected our plans for making the attempt.

I was to select a pilot and crew from the prisoners, and he agreed to arrange for our exit from the stockade. We kept up daily communication with each other until all was in readiness.

I had found a pilot and crew to man the boat. The capture seemed an easy job, as we would most likely find the guards asleep. We had accumulated some rations for the trip, and it was settled as to what night the start would be made.

The stockade was made with two-inch planks, twelve feet long, placed on end on the ground and strongly braced. The soil was sandy.

When the appointed time came our party quietly went to the place which had been selected for the work, and we were busily digging our way out, under the fence, when someone *inside* of the stockade reported us to the sergeant at the gate, who yelled out:

"Sergeant of the guard! Prisoners escaping!"

The sentinel on whose beat we were to escape could do no less than fire his gun, which he promptly did, and the bullet came through the fence at about the proper distance above the ground to perforate the body of anyone not lying down. It seemed almost a miracle that no one in our party of eight was hit.

All was confusion in short order, and it is needless to say that our party left for a better neighborhood. When a file of soldiers ultimately appeared on the scene they found almost everyone up and asking questions; but the parties who had drawn the fire of the sentry were among those sleeping peacefully in their quarters and dreaming of a home without rebel guards.

Added to the keen disappointment which we experienced over the frustrated effort to escape, we had the usual regrets incident to the failure of a business operation, for that boat and cargo in New Orleans would have meant a snug little pile to divide, and in this respect my own regrets were above the average felt by the crowd, for it had been agreed upon by the party that the rebel manager and myself should have an extra share of the spoils if the plan should be a success. By the law of compensation, or of force, he and I now had the lion's share of the disappointment.

With the sentinel a party to our escape and one of us as well, the thing had seemed so easy that, speaking for myself at least, we had in imagination seen ourselves, with bulging pockets, at home with our loved ones.

Our feelings can better be imagined than described.

It was always one of the mysteries of life to me how any prisoner could deliberately betray his comrades, and almost as much of a mystery how schemes of escape became known to others.

CHAPTER XXIII.

TO CAMP FORD AND JOY.

While we were in Shreveport my regiment was exchanged, and marched through on its way home. I tried very hard to be allowed to go with them, but Captain Burchard, who was in charge, refused to allow it. I had quite a row with him after pleadings and diplomacy had failed, but nothing did any good. It was decided that I must go back to Tyler on account of my two attempts to escape.

Shortly after this bitter disappointment the stockade got too full, and a lot of us were sent to Tyler under a heavy guard, Captain Rummel being left behind on account of sickness. These guards had special orders to shoot me if I tried to escape, evidently the result of my row with Captain Burchard. This fact was told to me by one of the guards, but I joked about it and professed not to believe it.

One of the guards was a boy, who seemed more inclined to general conversation than the rest. He walked and talked with me a good deal. In one of our talks he mentioned that he was from "Kasseder," in Davis county. As I knew several people in the place, having stopped there on my former return to Tyler, I at once surprised him by airing my knowledge. As I desired to amuse myself by quizzing him, I was mysterious and non-committal. He was puzzled considerably, and went off and told his captain.

The officer rode up to my side a little later and entered into a conversation. I treated him the same as I had treated the boy, and when he left me he was almost overpowered with curiosity.

I now discovered that one of the guards was the man whom I had met with a wagon when we crossed the Sulphur Fork of Red River. We talked together, but he did not recognize me. At first I claimed to have seen him before, but he thought not. After bothering him to my heart's content, I reminded him of our having crossed Sulphur Fork together, when he said that he had been suspicious of us at the time. This was so much of the "I-told-you-so" order that I had a good laugh at him for his "hindsight."

The other officers kept dropping back to interview me, and I got their curiosity inflamed to a high degree by talking familiarly of different places and of an imaginary plan of an underground railroad. This caused the officers to become agitated, and I saw that they suspected me of something serious. When a detail was finally sent to take me before the officer in command I concluded that the matter had gone far enough, and, when questioned, I explained how

I had become acquainted, on a previous runaway trip, with the people and places spoken of so familiarly. The matter ended in much laughter and some jokes.

During the rest of the march I talked negro suffrage and equality, at times nearly driving our captors wild by picturing the pleasures to come to them when these liberties should prevail. They got mad at times, but seemed to like hearing me talk, and evidently saw that I said more than I meant in some ways; yet I told many truths—which made them mad—about the actual practice by Southern whites of equality with negroes, as evidenced by the thousands of mulattoes among them.

Another source of amusement to me was to bother the guard at night by sleeping away from my companions and as near the guard line as I could. The guards would remonstrate and get mad, but I would blarney them a little and say that I had money on my person which I was afraid my companions would steal, and that I wanted to keep close to them for protection. They could not reasonably object to this, but it made them keep an eye on me in particular, and the various characteristics of the different men were a constant source of study and amusement.

My feelings on this journey were of a kind that kept me constantly on the "*qui vive*" for something to divert my mind from reflections.

To have escaped twice and been recaptured each time was bad enough, especially when one venture had been so nearly a success, and the failure through treachery of the last attempt to get away had seemed to cap the climax at the time; but to see all my regimental comrades file before me on their way to home and friends, while I was sent back to confinement, was the proverbial last straw—only, in this case, it did not break the camel's back; but it was a close call.

I had no interests in Camp Ford that I was not entirely willing to sacrifice for the sake of being at home or with my men, and the Confederacy was welcome to my rations if they would dispense with my presence; but, while my residence in Texas, with free board and lodging, was insisted upon so strongly as being necessary for the good of the country, I really could not leave the good people, not even for the sake of personal pleasures.

Talking to myself in this way when reflections crowded upon me, and by seizing every opportunity to amuse myself at the expense of the guards, I got the camel's back in pretty fair shape again, and resigned myself to the inevitable.

We finally reached the familiar stockade at Tyler, and about 250 of us were in line when we fell in for roll-call. Each man entered the stockade alone as his name was called.

As before described, the entrance of prisoners

was a noisy occasion, and one scene was very much like another; but, when I stepped into the enclosure, there was a movement of surprise and then a dead silence. Most of the men knew me, and their knowledge was communicated quickly to the rest. Seeing me come in after my long absence, and after my regiment had been exchanged, caused a sympathy that brought about silence almost as if by command.

I was not feeling particularly joyful anyway, and had had hard work to keep up my spirits on the road, so that this evidence of sympathy nearly caused me to break down altogether.

Soon after my return to the stockade I gained the title of Exchange Commissioner. I was familiar with the forms of all passes, furloughs, etc., and, as before stated, I could imitate almost any handwriting. As the new men in the place became acquainted with me and my accomplishments I was besieged with requests for different papers that would facilitate egress or escape.

The older prisoners were not as anxious for escape as the younger, or, rather, newer ones, as they had seen so many failures and punishments that they wanted a pretty sure thing before they risked an attempt.

Men even went so far as to ask me to get them out of the stockade, but I told them that I would give any papers they wanted, leaving to them the getting out.

My exchange or furlough business was conducted about as follows:

A man would come to me for the means of escape, or, rather, the means of avoiding recapture after escape. I would make out a written application from him to his captain for a leave of ten, twenty or thirty days, in which was stated the necessity for his going home to Upshur county, Texas, to procure clothing, which all Confederate soldiers then needed. On the back of this application would appear the approval of his captain, colonel and brigade commander, as well as the final and effective endorsement of Kirby Smith's adjutant, General Boggs, all the endorsements being made by me, except that of General Boggs, which was completely counterfeited by the adjutant of the 77th Ohio. Thus being fortified with legal authority to return to his regiment on an expired furlough, the prisoner would endeavor to appear as a dutiful Confederate soldier going to the front, get out as best he could, after receiving careful instructions as to his route and actions, and take his chances of success.

My escapes and experiences were talked over, and the men seemed to think that I could do most anything desired, the accidental character of our captures not being regarded as any reflection upon my ability in the attempts to escape.

A Colonel Jamison was now the commander of the stockade, and the officer who brought us in related to him some of my talks about negro suffrage and equality, which amused him very much.

One day he sent for me to come to him in order that he might hear some of my talk on these subjects. I evaded the topics as well as I could, but made so good an impression upon him that he gave me a pass to go in and out at will, with twenty men, upon my promise that I would not take advantage of it to escape myself or let any of my companions do so. My excuse for asking it was that we wanted to swim in the stream near by, gather wild greens and take proper exercise.

A few days later, as ten men and myself were in swimming under this pass in a creek about half a mile from the stockade we saw a couple of young negro boys watching us. I told the men to go ahead with their fun while I talked with the boys. One of these youngsters was about fourteen years old and the other nineteen. They knew who I was and all about my escapes, and were anxious to see me get away, urging me to break away right then, as there was no guard around, but I told them that I was out on parole and could not. They then told me that they had charge of the horses of the major at headquarters, and that I could at any time have a horse and uniform to help me get away, showing me the cabin where they lived and where I could come for this assistance.

I told the boys that I would take the first chance I had to get out without breaking parole, and they left me. I was greatly excited at the prospect, for I now knew the country so well that I had little fear of not being able to make my way to Little Rock with such assistance as I knew I could get along the road.

When we went back to the stockade I prepared some despatches from Kirby Smith to Gano, and planned the whole route and system which I would follow in general. My plan was simply to get out at night, get my uniform and horse, and ride for Dooley's Ferry as a despatch-bearer, taking my chances on my presence of mind being sufficient to carry me through in any emergency.

Recollecting all that had been said to me by Captain Payne—the guard who had let me ride his horse just after leaving Arkadelphia on the return trip—I figured that I could make Little Rock in about five days by hard riding, stopping here and there on the way to feed and rest, and having an easy time after reaching Dooley's Ferry.

The negro boy promised to keep the loss of the horse covered as long as possible, by pretending that the animal had gotten loose and strayed away, so that it was reasonable to assume that enough time would be spent in hunting the animal to render futile any pursuit from the stockade after my leave of absence became known to the guards. My despatches should take care of any ordinary obstacle in my way to the river, and, with my ability to "bluff" the average person or persons likely to be met, I felt confident that only an accident or extraordinary stoppage could upset my plans. Dooley would know me when I referred to Captain Payne, and my passage of Red River was assured if I reached that point, while he would also direct me to the captain's place, some ten or fifteen miles away, where I would be certain of concealment and assistance. The captain's neighbor, who had sons in the Federal army, would find a way to get me within our lines, with the assistance of horses from Payne's corral. Altogether, I could almost see myself at home again.

The thing was feasible, and I was anxious to try it, scarcely being able to sleep at nights for thinking about it.

The men about me all tried to dissuade me on account of the risk of capture with a horse in my possession, and because Lee had surrendered and the war could not last much longer, saying that I was foolish to take any risks at such a time.

There was much talk at this time, among the rebels, of Kirby Smith's holding out in the Southwest and being heavily reinforced by the scattered remnants of other armies. This had an appearance of being reasonable, as matters then looked to us, and I would listen to no arguments against my proposed scheme; so a day was set for my departure, and I fully intended to go.

When I was sufficiently well supplied with food and really ready to start, my companions begged and pleaded with me so hard not to risk it till we were more certain of continued imprisonment that I compromised by postponing the date.

This thing went on for several weeks, I making postponement after postponement, until I finally settled it decidedly that I would go on such a day unless we got some favorable news.

Before the fixed time came around we saw Captain Burchard ride by the stockade and go to headquarters. Knowing that he was after some more prisoners for exchange, we sent out a man to learn who were to be the favored ones. The messenger came back, all in a flutter of excitement, and announced that all were to go.

The scene of confusion and excitement which ensued cannot be described. The men simply went wild. For myself, I had to sit down to quiet my nervousness.

The guards began to leave for home as soon as the news became known. Twenty-four hours after Captain Burchard arrived there were no guards to be seen anywhere, except the higher officers, and we could have broken out any time after that. We were not silly enough to do this, however, as it would have relieved the rebels too much, for they were bound to feed and escort us if we stayed.

We were kept three days in the stockade, awaiting the arrival of rations, and during this time we had no regular food, as the mill which the rebels had used to grind grain had broken down just at a time when they seemed to need it most.

The citizens flocked in to see us, and brought us food, or we should have gone hungry during this interval. They came to trade for the things which we would leave behind us, and we sold off the pots and kettles belonging to the Confederacy, until the authorities learned the fact and placed a guard at the gate to prevent any further depletion of their stock of cooking utensils. As the prisoners now had nothing to cook, they commenced to break up and throw into the cesspools all that was left of the cooking outfit, and before long there was not a pot or skillet to be found.

By this time the stockade was broken in several places, and we could pass in and out at will, but it was more the desire to feel that we could do so which prompted any egress than any desire to go anywhere, as we were all anxious to get home, and did not want to go by ourselves when all were going so soon.

An irrepressible Zouave prisoner got into the headquarters room one day, and, filled with enthusiasm and the conviction that the Confedcracy was busted, nearly destroyed the records in the office before he was discovered and kicked out.

Finally, the rations not coming, the rebels got an ox-team with which to haul the sick men, and we made a start for Shreveport.

It is a matter of record that I was the last man to leave the stockade on this occasion, and consequently the last prisoner confined in it. I made it a point to see that every other human being was out of the enclosure before I departed, and to have others know the fact. I will not attempt to describe my feelings as the final exit was made; suffice it to say that it was one of the happiest moments of my life.

CHAPTER XXIV.

LIBERTY AT LAST.

On the second day out from the stockade, and before reaching Marshall, we came to a house where a farmer was offering to trade for blankets. Mine was on a horse at the head of the procession, but I had a ten-cent "shinplaster," with which I bought some biscuits of the man. He had two loads of blankets piled up close by, which he had already secured by trading, and he had some wine in bottles for further use.

I was very anxious to possess some of that wine, and I hustled around among the prisoners and borrowed a blanket from a young fellow who was willing to take my word that I would return it or give him mine when we caught up with the leaders of our band. I secured three bottles of wine for the blanket, and we had some refreshments, eating the biscuits and drinking the wine until there was no more left.

As we hurried on to catch up I saw a pile of blankets near the fence, and I at once returned the boy's blanket to him in the shape of a better one, taken from this pile.

The next morning I gave myself permission to leave the rest of the outfit and forage on ahead, which I kept up till we reached Four Mile Springs, where I arrived thirty-six hours ahead of the main body.

Here I found a lot of Smith's men who had deserted, and who were red hot for Sherman to call for troops to go to Mexico for the purpose of clearing out Maximilian, who was just then usurping authority. These men were not nursing resentment against their opponents in our war, but would have hailed with joy any enterprise in which Federals and Confederates could stand shoulder to shoulder, for, as they expressed it, "the combination would sweep the earth."

Going on to Shreveport, I found everything in a chaotic condition. There were batteries without horses, officers without men, and most of the stores had been looted by the departing troops.

We were two days about town, awaiting transportation, and saw that every horse that came within range was confiscated by soldiers, even to stopping wood wagons in the road and taking the animals away from them, the soldiers then leaving for home.

There was much expectation of seeing some of the Union fleet come up the river as transports, but they did not put in an appearance, and the citizens of the town were nearly frantic in consequence, on account of the plundering that was being done. During a conversation with several gentlemen, who were eager to ascertain what was known of the possible coming of the fleet, they told me that only the coming of the Federal army could save them from total financial ruin. The actions of these men were in accordance with their words, and, apparently, they voiced the sentiments of the entire business community.

The Confederate soldiers, realizing that the war was practically over, and being in need of nearly everything, made no apologies for the liberties taken, but, on the principle that "might makes right," appropriated everything in sight that was likely to be of use to them in solving the problem of how to live after peace had been declared. The situation, while full of excitement for all, had its amusing aspect, and I thought of it as another illustration of the fact that "those who dance must pay the fiddler."

Early in our march from the stockade I had had my sympathy greatly excited by the increasing illness of one of the sick men. His birthplace and residence had been in Pennsylvania, but he had gone over the State line and enlisted in the 3d Maryland. He had been sick for some time previous to our departure from the stockade, and had grown rapidly worse while on the road, despite the stimulation of being on his way to home and friends. He had been so brave and cheerful, notwithstanding his youthful age of only eighteen years, that I had become much interested in him. While prostrated on his bed of cotton, he had talked to me of his home and mother, and had spoken bravely of his chances of dying. With a bright look on his face, he had said:

"I may pull through, Captain, and I may not; but I won't give up till I have to, for mother needs me; only I want you to let her know if anything happens."

I had done what I could for the boy, and on several occasion had gotten him milk and other things. He had given me his mother's name and address, but the absence of writing material at the time had prevented the making of other than a mental memorandum, and the necessity for a better record had been overlooked in the confusion and excitement of the trip. When the main body of our command caught up with me at Shreveport I was shocked to learn that he was dead. I had had doubts as to his living to get home, but so early a death was a surprise and shock, which latter was turned to self-reproach and sorrow when I found that I could not recollect the name and address given to me.

Fifteen years afterward, during which time I frequently tried in vain to recollect the data necessary to identify him, the name, address and other knowledge suddenly came to me one day when I was not thinking about it. At once I sat down and wrote to the mother, and in due time received a beautiful letter in reply. My letter was the first word she had received of the boy since he had last written to her in good health and spirits, except that the books of his company bore his name, with an "absent without leave" score against it. I recollected that he had told me of his having slipped off to forage a little on his own account at the time of his capture. Making an affidavit of the facts as I knew them, I sent it to her, and the pension which she could not get upon the records as they stood was promptly allowed her on the affidavit furnished.

After waiting for the Federal transports until tired, our guards placed us on a couple of rebel boats, and we started down the river for the Yankee fleet.

I was on the boat with Colonel Samansky, a Pole. He had been an officer in his own country, had enlisted in the Confederate army, and had gained the rank of Colonel. He lived in Texas and expected to remain there. When he asked me how I had been treated, the only complaint that I could consistenly make against those having me in charge was that I had not been exchanged with my regiment. I claimed to him that I had been of more service to the Union as a prisoner than I could have been if I had remained in the service, as I had kept, on an average, two men busy watching me ever since I had been captured. I showed him some samples of my work as exchange commissioner, and purposely magnified the matter. He only laughed and complimented me upon my enterprise, he being the rebel exchange commissioner.

At the mouth of the Red River we met some Federal boats coming up with prisoners. While exchanging boats, all who desired it had a chance to take a swim, and a number of us enjoyed the luxury. Possibly 500 men were in the water at one time.

One notable feature of this occasion was the fact remarked by everyone that you could tell a Yankee from a rebel as far as you could see him, even without his clothes. The reason for this was that our confinement in the open air had caused us to be burned brown by the sun, even through our clothing, while the rebels were white from confinement within walls.

We were taken down to New Orleans and housed there ten days in a cotton press, arriving on Sunday afternoon in our prison garb. We were a rather hard-looking crowd, but never was there a happier one.

The boys in New Orleans knew that we were coming, and Capt. S. H. Harper, formerly a sergeant in my company, hunted me up and took me home with him. He was there on a detail, and was delighted to see me. I was fed on the best he had, and arrayed in a spare uniform of his. When I went back to the cotton press the boys did not know me.

From the time of my capture to that of my arrival in New Orleans I had only once been able to get word through to my wife, and I wrote to her as soon as I had a chance to do so after reaching that place. My first knowledge of her, after my capture, was acquired through Captain Harper, who told me that she was well when he had heard from home the last time, and also told me that she had heard of me through an escaped prisoner.

All the officers crowded about the paymaster's office in New Orleans, trying to get some money, and he had quite a time with them, as, while he believed what they told him of themselves, he could pay out no money until some person known to him would vouch for the recipient.

Captain Harper satisfactorily identified me to the paymaster, and I drew two months' pay. A proper voucher was now easily secured by as many of the officers as were personally known to me, and all such received a like amount.

While in New Orleans I met Honeycut on the street. I had left him in the Washington guardhouse, confined as a spy. We spent the day together, and I learned his later story, as follows:

"Two days after you left they started me off south alone, giving me orders to report to Kirby Smith, but it didn't take me long to discover that they had a spy on my track. When I reached Smith's headquarters and told my story they allowed me to go on to Matamoras, but somebody would overtake me every day and try to pump me. I bluffed 'em all off, and kept on my way in a natural manner, getting through all right, but I didn't lose any time, after I once got clear, in getting here by water to report.

"Had a funny little experience on the way; worth telling. A woman I know, up in Ohio, gave me the address of her brother in Texas before I left, in case I got down that way. I hunted him up on my way down, and told him a fairy story about my being the woman's husband and her being in Matamoras, bringing in what I told you in Washington and spinning him a long yarn about my treatment while trying to join my wife. Guess he believed me—looked like it, anyhow, for he treated me royally and let me have two hundred and fifty in gold."

When we left New Orleans we were put on a boat and started up the river for Benton Barracks, St. Louis. When we landed at the mouth of White river we were allowed to go on shore for an hour or two, and I then learned that my regiment was up the river at Duval's Bluffs. I did not go on board again, and the boat left without me.

After spending two days among the mosquitoes of that region I at last secured transportation and started up the river to join my regiment. We had to be convoyed by a gunboat.

When I reached Duval's Bluffs my company was doing guard duty. I found all hands and had a great reception, learning all the home news. This was the first positive information of a recent date, about home matters, received by me since my capture.

After spending three or four days with the boys, I went home, and my wife and myself renewed our acquaintance.

She had heard of me through an escaped prisoner, who had reported me as being in the stockade, but she had received no other information concerning me until the boys had gotten home after the exchange. My letter from New Orleans had been a very welcome missive.

My friends at home flocked to see me, and I was kept busy telling my story.

Having gone through it all, I was disposed to drop the hardships from the story, except when questioned, and to treat the thing as a huge picnic. My natural disposition being to see the bright side only, the hardships of which I had to tell were made to have another aspect than the usual one presented of prison life. As a consequence of this fact, my story differed considerably from that of a number who had been prisoners with me.

Friends would come to me and hear my story, frequently saying:

"My! Swiggett, you do not seem to have had such a bad time of it. The others tell such horrible stories that it is a relief to hear yours; and yet you were in the same prison. How is it?"

I replied in such cases that most of my time as a prisoner had been spent outside of the stockade, in one way or another, and that, aside from the monotony and the separation from family, we did not see much more hardship than comes in the every-day life of lots of people out of prison, and that there was a bright side to it all.

"But you don't damn the rebels, Swiggett, like the others," they would say, to which I would reply that the rebels had treated me as well as they could under the circumstances, and that when people did the best they could they should not be damned for what they failed to do, especially as prison life was necessarily a hardship at its best.

There were cases of personal ill-treatment which came under my notice, but they were the great exceptions, and, as a rule, the rebels of my acquaintance did for their prisoners all that was possible with the means in their power, and treated them as well as prisoners could expect to be treated.

It may be of interest to the reader to learn that all the men who were my companions in escape are still living, except Capt. J. B. Gedney and Adjt. Stephen K. Mahon.

The rebels did not treat us as well as we might have been treated, as it was possible for Jeff Davis to have invited us to Richmond, arrayed us in his Sunday clothes, fed us at his own table and confined us in his front parlor. It may have been only an oversight that he did not do so, but it was not expected, and we harbored no ill-feelings because of the neglect. On the other hand, we were not treated as badly as we might have been, inasmuch as we were not deprived of companionship, and, as a rule, were allowed to sleep when we pleased, to rest as much as we desired, to be late for dinner if we wished, and to eat in our shirt sleeves without protest. Many a man is deprived of these privileges in his own home, and I have eaten food of a less nourishing character than that given us by the rebels, even at the table of a newly-married couple, where perfect bliss should reign supreme.

The war is over. Our foes had neither our resources nor our advantages in its prosecution, and many things that were easy for us were impossible for them. Abuse of authority is not a trait of man, but of men, and those who are indirectly responsible should not be too harshly censured for what they cannot altogether control. Incidents by the thousand of heroic, heart-touching actions performed for humanity's sake during our war by those on one side for those on the other reflect as much credit upon rebels as upon Yankees, and I have always felt that, on the whole, our antagonists did the best they could for their prisoners.

THE END.

APPENDIX.

Brief Sketches of my Companions.

FRANCIS MARION DRAKE, GOVERNOR OF IOWA.

The parents of Governor Drake were John Adams Drake and Mrs. Harriet O'Neil Drake. They were natives of the Old North State; removed to Rushville, Ill., where the son, Francis Marion, was born December 30, 1830. From Rushville they removed to Fort Madison, Iowa, in the fall of 1837. The father was a merchant in Illinois, but served as judge of probate of Lee county, Iowa, when a resident of Fort Madison, until the spring of 1846. He then removed to Davis county, Iowa, and founded the village of Drakeville. Francis Marion received his early education in the common schools, and also acquired a knowledge of law.

When the gold excitement in California was at its height he crossed the plains in 1852 with ox-teams, and again in 1854 with a drove of cattle. On the first trip across, his company of sixteen men had a severe engagement with the Pawnees at Shell Creek, Neb., in which they encountered about 300 Indians, who were defeated with heavy loss and driven across the Platte river. On his return from California, October 1, 1854, he was a passenger on the ill-fated steamer "Yankee Blade," which was wrecked and totally lost, and he was picked up five days later on a barren coast which he had succeeded in reaching.

He had been successful in his California ventures, and on the 1st of January, 1855, entered the mercantile business with his father, and brother, J. H. Drake, under the firm name of Drake & Sons, at Drakeville. In June, 1861, he enlisted as a private in the volunteer service of the United States and served until the close of the war, being promoted to captain, major, lieutenant-colonel and from lieutenant-colonel to the rank of brigadier-general by brevet. He was in many severe engagements, in one of which he was seriously, at first thought mortally, wounded, and from which wound he has never entirely recovered. His record for bravery and efficiency was universally commended by his superior officers, and his military career is one of which he may well be proud.

On resuming civil life, General Drake engaged in the practice of law, in which he was eminently successful, for a period of three years, when he entered the railroad business, organizing and building what is now known as the Keokuk & Western Railroad. He resumed his law practice for another period of three years, associated with Gen. A. J. Baker, who became attorney-general of the State, when he again entered upon the railroad business, and has organized and built by his own efforts over 400 miles of railroad, a large part of which he still controls, being president of the Indiana, Illinois & Iowa, Albia & Centerville and director in the Iowa Central and Keokuk & Western railroads. He has also been successful as a banker, and is president of the Centerville National Bank.

His material interests have not prevented him from taking an active interest in educational matters and missionary work. He is president of the board of trustees of Drake University, at Des Moines, named after him, on account of his great liberality to that institution in its building and endowment. He has also been a contributor to many other educational institutions.

In 1895 he accepted the nomination of the republican party for Governor of the State of Iowa, and was elected by a large majority, having received the largest vote ever given for a candidate for Governor of the State.

On the 24th of December, 1855, he was married to Mary Jane Lord, who died on the 22d day of June, 1883. He has six children, four daughters and two sons. The daughters are Amelia, Jennie, Eva, and Mary Lord; the sons, Frank Ellsworth and John Adams.

Amelia is the wife of T. P. Shonts, of Chicago, general manager of the Indiana, Illinois & Iowa Railroad; Jennie is the wife of Dr. J. L. Sawyers, of Centerville, Iowa; Eva is the wife of Henry Goss, wholesale and retail boot and shoe merchant, of Centerville, Iowa; Mary Lord is the wife of George W. Sturdivant, banker, at Moravia, Iowa. Frank Ellsworth is president of the Centerville Block Coal Co., of Centerville, Iowa; John Adams is secretary and treasurer of the Indiana, Illinois & Iowa Railroad Co., of Chicago.

Governor Drake's photograph is inserted opposite page 18.

CAPTAIN THOMAS M. FEE.

Thomas Milton Fee was born at Feesburg, Brown county, Ohio, on April 18, 1839. His father was Thomas J. Fee, who was of English ancestry and a native of Virginia, and his mother's maiden name was Sarah Hastings, she being of Irish descent and born in Pennsylvania. His father laid out the town of Feesburg.

The son began an independent career at the age of nineteen, by finding occupation as a school-teacher. In a short time he went to Ottumwa, Iowa, and began to read law. Early in 1862 he was admitted to the bar, and the following spring he located in Centerville, Iowa, and began the practice of his profession. For two years, while reading law, he was principal of city schools at Ottumwa.

In August, 1862, he enlisted as a private in Company G of the 36th Iowa Infantry, and in October was the choice of his company for captain, receiving his commission from Governor Stone. He served with his command until captured at Marks' Mills with the writer and the rest of the brigade, and was a prisoner at Tyler, Texas, for ten months, except while absent without leave. After his exchange he was on detached service; first as Assistant Inspector-General of the Trans-Mississippi Department, and afterwards as Inspector of the Seventh Army Corps. When discharged at the close of the war he returned to Centerville, Iowa, and permanently entered upon the practice of law. In 1874 he was elected District Attorney of the Second Judicial District of Iowa for the term of four years, and Judge of the same district. He is a married man, and has five living children, three sons and two daughters. His photograph is inserted opposite page 89.

CAPTAIN B. F. MILLER.

B. F. Miller was born in Mount Pleasant, Westmoreland county, Pennsylvania, on October 2, 1832, of native parents, but of English and Scotch descent, his father being Benjamin Miller, and his mother's maiden name being Martha Hemphill. His business was farming until four years before the war, when he went west, spending two years of the four in the Rocky Mountains.

Coming east again, he enlisted at Wooster, Ohio, in Company D of the 120th Ohio Infantry, and served as private, sergeant, first lieutenant and captain. He was captured on May 3, 1864, at Shaggy Point, on the Red River, in Louisiana, and was imprisoned at Camp Ford, Texas, except during the attempt to escape, until exchanged on June 1, 1865. He was mustered out at Columbus, Ohio, on June 30, 1865.

On September 26, 1865, he married Julia A., sister of L. S. Baumgardner, of Toledo, Ohio, and farmed in that State until about three years ago, when rheumatic afflictions caused his cessation of active work. He then moved to Wooster, Ohio, where he now lives with his family, having but one child, a daughter. It is unnecessary to say more of Captain Miller, as he is mentioned frequently elsewhere. His photograph is inserted opposite page 167.

CAPTAIN J. P. RUMMEL.

J. P. Rummel was born in Worthington township, Richfield county, Ohio, on February 7, 1840, and worked in the blacksmith shop of his father until he was eighteen years of age. He was the son of Peter and Susanna Rummel. Qualifying as a teacher, he began work as such in a district school, and was so engaged when the first call was made for troops to put down the rebellion.

He enlisted as a private in Company I of the 16th Ohio Infantry, was in the first two engagements in Western Virginia, and was regularly discharged on August 18 of the same year. He re-enlisted on August 4, 1862, in Company B of the 120th Ohio Infantry, and became a second lieutenant before leaving camp. After the engagements at Chickasaw Bayou and Arkansas Post he was promoted to a captaincy on March 14, 1863, and was with his regiment in the campaign of Vicksburg and in part of the Red River campaign, being captured in December, 1864, while en route up the river with an expedition to reinforce General Banks at Alexandria. He was sent to Camp Ford, Texas, for imprisonment, escaped with the writer, as described elsewhere, was taken sick at Shreveport, La., after being recaptured, and remained there until the close of the war, being finally discharged from the army on June 29, 1865.

On his return home he became a clerk in a hardware store, and continued at this occupation for about a year and a half, during which time he married Miss Eva R. Redrup, of Mansfield, Ohio. In 1867 he engaged in business for himself in Mansfield, and is now the principal proprietor of a manufacturing establishment there. He has four living children. His photograph is inserted opposite page 115.

ADJUTANT S. K. MAHON.

Stephen Keith Mahon was born in Ireland on June 30, 1838. He was the son of John and Sarah Mahon, and his father was a gentleman farmer and merchant in the old country. The family came to the United States in 1849, living in Green County, Ohio, for five years, and then moving to Ottumwa, Iowa. At the outbreak of the war Stephen was employed in a general store at Blakesburg, Iowa.

He enlisted when the 36th Iowa Infantry was organized, was appointed sergeant-major at the staff organization, and was commissioned adjutant in August, 1863, in which capacity he served until mustered out at the close of the war. He participated in all the skirmishes and battles of his regiment up to the time of his capture with the writer at Marks' Mills, having been breveted captain for gallantry in the battle of Helena, Ark. His unsuccessful attempt to escape with the writer is elsewhere recorded, and he remained a prisoner at Camp Ford until regularly exchanged about the close of the war.

In February, 1866, he received a second lieutenant's commission in the regular army, and was assigned to the 11th U. S. Infantry. In July, 1866, he was promoted, and again in July, 1882, becoming a captain in the 16th Infantry at the latter date. His services in Virginia, Mississippi and Louisiana during the reconstruction period were highly creditable, and he was at one time ordered by President Grant to Washington for personal interview on reconstruction matters in Mississippi.

The hardships of prison life sowed the seeds of the disease which caused his death, and in August, 1879, he was compelled to go home from Fort Sill, Indian Territory, on a sick leave, which was extended until he was placed as captain on the retired list of the army in 1883. He was a great sufferer from the time of his sick leave until his death, which occurred at his home on January 11, 1885. Even at the last he loved to hear again and talk of the old stories of the camp.

Our adjutant never married. He was a brother of Maj. Samuel Mahon, of Ottumwa, Iowa; Capt. William Mahon, of Cincinnati, Ohio, and Mrs. Col. C. W. Kittredge, of Trinidad, Col. Another sister lives in Ottumwa. Adjutant Mahon was a high-minded, honorable gentleman and a true friend. His picture is inserted opposite page 69.

CAPTAIN CHARLES BURNBAUM.

Charles Burnbaum was born in Lockport, Ohio, on February 16, 1834, of German parentage, his father having emigrated in 1824 and later married a German lady in Ohio. Young Burnbaum started out for himself at the age of sixteen, and learned the trade of harness-making at New Philadelphia, Ohio. Later he moved to Eddyville, Iowa, where he engaged in merchandising until the time of his enlistment in the army.

In 1862 he became a member of Company D of the 36th Iowa Infantry, and was elected lieutenant. He participated in all the marches and engagements of his company and his regiment until the time of his capture with the writer at Marks' Mills, Arkansas, in 1864, and was a prisoner at Camp Ford, Texas, except during the attempt to escape, until regularly exchanged about the close of the war. He was made captain on his return to his company.

After being mustered out in 1865 he located in Marshalltown, Iowa, and a few years later moved to Chicago, becoming a commercial traveler. He afterwards engaged in the hardware business at Milan, Mo., and in 1878 he married Miss Kate Gilmore. His present residence is Hot Springs, Ark., where he is successfully engaged in the wholesale grocery business. His photograph is inserted opposite page 94.

CAPTAIN JAMES B. GEDNEY.

James B. Gedney was born in Dearborn county, Indiana, on December 10, 1825. In 1838 he removed to Lee county, Iowa, and there, in 1848, he married Miss Sarah Linch. Five years later he removed to Appanoose county, Iowa, and became one of its foremost citizens in every enterprise for the good of the community, being one of the first settlers in that section. In 1859, during the gold excitement, he made a brief trip across the plains to what was then known as "the Pike's Peak country."

In 1862 he enlisted as a private, was elected captain, and he and his comrades were assigned as Company I of the 36th Iowa Infantry. He participated with his command in all its campaigns and engagements until captured with the writer at Marks' Mills, and remained a prisoner at Tyler, Texas, except during the attempt to escape, until regularly exchanged about the close of the war.

On his return home after the war he again took up farming in Appanoose county, keeping at this until 1890, when he bought property in Centerville, the county-seat, and became a resident of that town. Captain Gedney held many positions of honor and trust, serving five years on the board of county supervisors and six years as president of his county's agricultural association, besides having the confidence of his neighbors in other ways.

The disease which caused his death was contracted in the army, and on July 27, 1893, he died at the age of sixty-eight years, honored and loved by all who knew him. His memory will live long in the hearts of his comrades, because of the soldierly and manly qualities that endeared him to all his associates. His photograph is inserted opposite page 79.

LIEUTENANT WALTER S. JOHNSON.

Walter S. Johnson was born in Union county, Indiana, near Liberty, on May 24, 1835. His ancestors were orthodox Quakers, and were early settlers near Lynchburg, Va., about 1690. About 1826 his grandparents moved to Cincinnati, Ohio, and a few years later to Liberty, Ind. When Walter was about fourteen the family located in Appanoose county, Iowa, and at the age of eighteen he built the first store in the new town of Cincinnati, Iowa, and began merchandising. In 1855 he married Sarah B., daughter of James X. Gibson, and is now the father of five living children.

On July 8, 1861, he enlisted in Company D of the 6th Iowa Infantry, under the Hon. M. M. Walden, and was assigned to General Fremont's command in Missouri. In July, 1862, he was discharged for disability caused by hard marching and exposure while recovering from an attack of the measles. The spirit of patriotism was too strong to permit inactivity after his recovery, and he again enlisted on August 11, 1862, reporting in person to Adjutant-General Baker with 100 men for duty, and being assigned as Company I of the 36th Iowa Infantry. He served with his command until captured with the writer, as elsewhere described.

While the regiment was at Camden, Ark., four days previous to the capture, George W. Gibson, a brother of Lieutenant Johnson's wife, came to Company I as a recruit, and was killed in the fight at Marks' Mills.

The lieutenant remained a prisoner, except as narrated elsewhere, until regularly exchanged about the close of the war. After being mustered out he returned home and resided on a farm of his until the fall of 1870, when he was elected Clerk of the District Court of Appanoose county, which position he filled for three terms. He was then elected Mayor of Centerville, Iowa, after which he again engaged in merchandising until the spring of 1890, when he moved to his present home in Lincoln, Neb., to be nearer his children. His photograph is inserted opposite page 39.

SERGEANT E. B. ROCKET.

E. B. Rocket was born on July 14, 1841, in Jefferson county, Alabama, and moved with his parents to Arkansas in 1852. In 1859 he married Amanda, daughter of Absalom Holcombe.

In 1863 he enlisted in the Confederate army, and served until the close of the war, gaining the rank of sergeant. He was a member of Company B, Munson's regiment, Cobbles's brigade, Fagan's division, and was with his company in all its marches and engagements.

His wife died in 1881, leaving five girls and one boy to the care of the father. In 1885 he married Martha J. Davis, a widow, and four girls have blessed this union. At the age of seventeen Rocket became a convert to the tenets of the Missionary Baptist Church, to which he still adheres, his present occupation being that of preacher in this church, with his home in Center Point, Arkansas.

The writer's first meeting with Sergeant Rocket is fully described in the body of this book, and, while the acquaintance was unsought, it resulted in a lasting friendship, our captor proving to be a good soldier and a Christian gentleman. His photograph is inserted opposite page 189.

APPENDIX.   243

The following is a list of casualties among the officers and enlisted men of the Thirty-sixth Iowa Infantry at Marks' Mills, Arkansas, April 25, 1864:

Colonel F. M. Drake, wounded and captured.
Major A. H. Hamilton, captured.
Surgeon Colin G. Strong, captured.
Assistant Surgeon Patrick A. Smyth, captured.
Adjutant Stephen K. Mahon, captured.
Chaplain Michael H. Hare, captured.

NON-COMMISSIONED STAFF.

Quartermaster Sergeant Barton A. Ogle, captured.
Commissary Sergeant David A. Stanton, captured.
Pr. Mus. Joseph Peach, captured.

COMPANY A.

Captain John M. Porter, captured.
First Sergeant Davison P. Bay, captured.
Sergeant Asa S. Baird, captured.
Sergeant Thomas G. Robb, mortally wounded and captured.
Corporal Charles S. Deyo, captured.
Corporal James Nickol, wounded and captured.
Corporal John Lucas, captured.
Private Benjamin Bennett, killed.
Private Peter Boyer, mortally wounded and captured.
Private Isaac Belles, killed.
Private Hezekiah M. Chidester, captured.
Private Thomas L. Castle, captured.
Private George O. Catron, wounded and captured.
Private William Castle, captured.
Private John M. Connett, captured.
Private John Dempsey, captured.
Private William H. Dean, captured.
Private Robert A. Dunn, captured.
Private Alexander Elder, wounded and captured.
Private John Foreman, captured.
Private Albert Grimes, wounded and captured.
Private George W. Grass, captured.

Private Jacob Hendrix, captured.
Private John Kritzer, captured.
Private Francis G. Livingston, captured.
Private George Lindsay, captured.
Private Robert Martin, mortally wounded and captured.
Private Sylvester Mefford, killed.
Private Joseph Madow, wounded and captured.
Private James McKissick, wounded and captured.
Private William E. McKissick, captured.
Private Almond McNeil, captured.
Private William Martin, captured.
Private Samuel F. Noel, captured.
Private David Parks, captured.
Private Daniel Shepherd, killed.
Private Darius Stacey, captured.
Private Grandison F. Stephenson, captured.
Private William F. Sperry, mortally wounded and captured.
Private John C. Taylor, captured.
Private Leander Tyrrel, captured.
Private Robert B. Thompson, wounded and captured.
Private Laurel H. Tyrrel, captured.
Private William W. Wills, captured.

COMPANY B.

Captain S. A. Swiggett, captured.
Lieutenant Josiah H. McVay, captured.
Sergeant John W. Woods, captured.
Sergeant James Gandy, captured.
Sergeant Thomas R. Cole, captured.
Corporal Benjamin F. Chisman, captured.
Private William I. Barker, killed.
Private Lucius Bond, wounded and captured.
Private John Barnes, captured.
Private Henry C. Brown, wounded and captured.
Private John N. Belles, captured.
Private Isaac N. Belles, killed.
Private Benjamin Carter, killed.
Private Lorenzo H. Case, captured.
Private Noyes Chisman, wounded and captured.
Private John W. Clark, captured.
Private Banion O. Custer, killed.
Private Thomas W. Crandall, captured.
Private Nelson Derby, captured.
Private Jesse Dutton, captured.
Private William C. Derby, captured.

Private Samuel W. Fail, captured.
Private James R. Fent, wounded and captured.
Private James H. Finley, wounded and captured.
Private Levi Gates, wounded and captured.
Private Daniel Good, captured.
Private Peter Good, wounded and captured.
Private John Harsbarger, killed.
Private Amos W. Kent, killed.
Private Daniel W. Kirkpatrick, killed.
Private Henry R. Kirkpatrick, captured.
Private Thomas McCormick, wounded and captured.
Private Josiah D. McVay, captured.
Private James S. Major, captured.
Private Richard W. Moore, captured.
Private George W. Olney, captured.
Private Hiram A. Pratt, captured.
Private John Pence, wounded and captured.
Private Israel H. Pollock, captured.
Private William P. Riley, captured.
Private John M. Rose, captured.
Private John W. Rubel, wounded and captured.
Private Charles W. Reece, captured.
Private Madison E. S. Rubel, captured.
Private Annon L. Silvey, captured.
Private Mordecai Scaggs, captured.
Private Albert Stevenson, captured.
Private William H. H. Scott, captured.
Private Eli A. Spain, captured.
Private Calvin H. Smith, wounded and captured.
Private Jacob West, captured.
Private Sanford C. West, captured.
Private Daniel W. Williams, wounded and captured.
Private David E. Williams, wounded and captured.
Private William West, captured.

COMPANY C.

Captain Allen W. Miller, captured.
Lieutenant W. F. Vermilyea, captured.
Sergeant Marion H. Skinner, captured.
Sergeant George W. Dean, wounded and captured.
Sergeant Benjamin S. Vierling, wounded and captured.
Corporal Jesse G. Dean, captured.
Corporal William F. Patterson, wounded and captured.
Corporal James H. Bovell, wounded and captured.
Fifer Christopher D. Conrad, wounded and captured.
Private Wilson Burris, captured.

Private Nathan I. Bray, captured.
Private Jesse Clark, wounded and captured.
Private Eli Cummings, mortally wounded and captured.
Private John P. Goodvin, wounded and captured.
Private Jacob A. Grubb, killed.
Private Cyrus S. Hedgecock, captured.
Private Lucien B. Hudgins, captured.
Private Samuel A. Hayes, wounded and captured.
Private Joshua Jones, captured.
Private Alexander Kennedy, wounded and captured.
Private Uriah Link, wounded and captured.
Private James Lamar, captured.
Private James A. Miller, killed.
Private William H. H. McKim, captured.
Private Elias Mitchell, captured.
Private Mathias McCoy, killed.
Private George Matherly, captured.
Private John McCoy, wounded and captured.
Private John W. Needham, killed.
Private Thomas B. Porter, killed.
Private Robert R. Polk, captured.
Private Alexander P. Primm, captured.
Private Thomas I. Robinson, captured.
Private William H. Riggle, captured.
Private Hugh G. W. Scott, captured.
Private Daniel H. Sumner, captured.
Private Isaac Smith, captured.
Private Andrew J. Stansberry, captured.
Private John A. Stansbury, mortally wounded and captured.
Private James R. Sumner, captured.
Private Cyrenias Thomas, mortally wounded and captured.
Private Michael K. Tedrow, captured.
Private Epraim Vandoon, captured.

COMPANY D.

Captain Thomas B. Hale, captured.
Lieutenant Charles Burnbaum, captured.
Sergeant Francis M. Eperson, captured.
Sergeant Hiram Underwood, captured.
Corporal Joseph Griflis, captured.
Corporal William L. Palmer, captured.
Corporal George W. Nicely, killed.
Corporal Peter Stuber, mortally wounded and captured.
Corporal Thomas West, captured.
Corporal Francis M. Dofflemyer, captured.
Fifer Joseph Peach, captured.

Private William Amos, captured.
Private James Anthony, captured.
Private Howard R. Allen, captured.
Private George W. Blair, captured.
Private Moses R. Butler, captured.
Private Watson W. Coder, wounded and captured.
Private Jacob F. Coder, captured.
Private Francis M. Crane, captured.
Private Lafayette Campbell, captured.
Private Andrew Crook, captured.
Private John D. Dofflemeyer, captured.
Private John S. Foster, captured.
Private Benjamin F. Gordon, captured.
Private John S. Gray, captured.
Private David Gushwa, captured.
Private William B. Griffis, captured.
Private Sylvester Hendrix, captured.
Private Anthony Jones, captured.
Private Mervin T. Keran, captured.
Private Leonard Knox, captured.
Private James Kavanaugh, captured.
Private Horace M. Lyman, killed.
Private Charles L. Ladd, mortally wounded and captured.
Private Charles E. Little, captured.
Private Abner W. Lyman, captured.
Private Franze Marquardt, captured.
Private William W. Mardis, captured.
Private John H. Miller, captured.
Private Hugh H. Miller, captured.
Private Daniel Myers, captured.
Private George Myers, captured.
Private Curtis Moffat, captured.
Private David F. Newsom, captured.
Private Lucian L. Parker, captured.
Private Henry Parish, captured.
Private John W. Robinson, captured.
Private David H. Robinson, captured.
Private Philip Sinclair, captured.
Private Christopher Sharon, captured.
Private Henry G. True, captured.
Private Abram Umbenhower, captured.
Private Harmon Varner, captured.
Private Andrew I. Willsey, captured.
Private Joseph G. Williams, wounded and captured.
Private Asberry Way, captured.
Private Peter Warner, wounded and captured.

COMPANY E.

No officer.
First Sergeant Henry Slagle, captured.
Sergeant Lewis Myers, Jr., mortally wounded and captured.
Corporal Elias Parke, wounded and captured.
Corporal Michael E. Jackson, wounded and captured.
Corporal George W. Dennis, captured.
Corporal Frederick Campbell, captured.
Corporal Peter Shearer, captured.
Corporal Edward C. Soper, captured.
Fifer Thomas Skinner, captured.
Private Henry Adcock, wounded and captured.
Private James G. D. Aumack, captured.
Private Joseph Bivin, captured.
Private John I. Chance, captured.
Private Carey N. Carson, captured.
Private Samuel D. Cooper, captured.
Private Samuel W. Campbell, captured.
Private John H. Decker, captured.
Private John Duffee, captured.
Private Thomas W. Fenton, wounded and captured.
Private Alonzo Garrison, captured.
Private John Harness, wounded and captured.
Private John Henderson, captured.
Private Greenville Hale, captured.
Private Hiram Hale, captured.
Private Henry C. Hale, captured.
Private Richard Jackson, captured.
Private William W. Jackson, captured.
Private Joseph Kigar, mortally wounded and captured.
Private Peter H. Loy, wounded and captured.
Private Joseph Leslie, captured.
Private William H. Leslie, captured.
Private George L. McMahon, captured.
Private Isaac Mathews, captured.
Private Jonathan Nelson, captured.
Private Joseph Peden, wounded and captured.
Private George W. Phillips, wounded and captured.
Private Frederick Rachke, captured.
Private Benjamin F. Randall, captured.
Private John C. Scully, captured.
Private Andrew J. Stanton, captured.
Private Elias Sheffer, captured.
Private Jesse B. Skinner, captured.
Private Charles A. Stadler, captured.
Private John W. Stadler, captured.

Private Jesse H. Thompson, captured.
Private John A. Vermeulen, wounded.
Private Francis M. Watkins, captured.
Private George E. H. Ward, killed.
Private David M. Wallace, mortally wounded and captured.
Private Thomas H. Wallace, wounded and captured.
Private Woodson Wallace, captured.

COMPANY F.

Captain William F. Vermillion, captured.
Lieutenant John W. May, captured.
Lieutenant John N. Wright, captured.
First Sergeant Wm. R. Davenport, wounded and captured.
Sergeant William R. Kemper, captured.
Corporal Reuben D. Fouts, captured.
Corporal William H. Shuterly, captured.
Corporal John T. Sheeks, captured.
Private David H. Barnhart, captured.
Private William Bartlett, captured.
Private John Clark, captured.
Private George C. Carpenter, wounded and captured.
Private John L. Clowser, captured.
Private Joel Curtis, killed.
Private John Davis, wounded and captured.
Private Andrew J. Day, captured.
Private Simon Ely, captured.
Private John M. Elgin, wounded and captured.
Private John Free, captured.
Private Joseph Y. Funkhouser, captured.
Private William H. Fuller, captured.
Private Stephen A. D. Fenton, captured.
Private Manoah Graham, wounded and captured.
Private Thomas Galbraith, wounded and captured.
Private Albert Gillman, mortally wounded and captured.
Private Henry Hontz, captured.
Private David Howell, wounded and captured.
Private James R. Huiatt, captured.
Private Bial D. Kines, captured.
Private Perry G. Luzader, wounded and captured.
Private Charles B. Main, killed.
Private Lewis Main, captured.
Private Levi McHenry, captured.
Private Ephraim Nicholson, wounded and captured.
Private William K. Neel, captured.
Private Greenberry Owen, wounded and captured.

Private Thomas W. Patrick, captured.
Private Wesley Perigo, mortally wounded and captured.
Private Daniel Peppers, captured.
Private Charles W. Ryckman, captured.
Private James H. Ryckman, mortally wounded and captured.
Private Samuel H. Smith, captured.
Private Henry H. Swift, captured.
Private David A. Stewart, wounded and captured.
Private John Standley, wounded and captured.
Private Parney S. Sullivan, wounded and captured.
Private John Whitset, captured.
Private John Wafford, captured.
Private Levi H. Zentz, captured.

COMPANY G.

Captain Thomas M. Fee, captured.
Lieutenant B. F. Pearson, captured.
First Sergeant Andrew J. Boston, captured.
Sergeant Nicholas Snedeker, captured.
Sergeant Silas A. Snider, captured.
Sergeant James S. Thompson, captured.
Sergeant James Thompson, captured.
Sergeant James A. Lowry, captured.
Corporal Francis M. Snider, captured.
Corporal Ezra Wade, killed.
Corporal James Lowrey, captured.
Corporal Willis Higgenbotham, captured.
Private Martin Benge, wounded and captured.
Private William I. Buck, captured.
Private Smith Bowen, mortally wounded and captured.
Private Eli Bryant, wounded and captured.
Private Isaac Beaman, captured.
Private James Bridgeman, captured.
Private Thomas Crage, captured.
Private George T. Cavanah, captured.
Private Michael Cridlebaugh, captured.
Private Isaac Cross, captured.
Private James G. Davison, captured.
Private James A. Douglass, captured.
Private William R. Fisk, wounded and captured.
Private John Gilbert, wounded and captured.
Private John R. Hodge, captured.
Private Francis Hall, captured.
Private Amos Hays, captured.
Private John Herring, wounded and captured.

Private M. W. Harney, wounded.
Private Newton Kirby, captured.
Private Simon Launtz, captured.
Private Amos Moiril, captured.
Private Enoch F. Mapes, captured.
Private John J. Morrison, captured.
Private William Morril, wounded and captured.
Private Arloff Maring, captured.
Private Harrison B. Masters, captured.
Private Wesley Mansfield, captured.
Private Robert B. Smith, captured.
Private Charles A. Staith, captured.
Private Samuel R. Shaw, captured.
Private William Thomas, captured.
Private William I. Zimmer, captured.

COMPANY H.

Lieutenant James M. Thompson, captured.
Corporal Darius T. Anderson, captured.
Corporal David H. Conger, captured.
Corporal Jacob Breon, captured.
Corporal John Archibald, captured.
Corporal Thomas Dyson, captured.
Corporal Isaac W. Powell, wounded and captured.
Corporal Levi Overman, wounded and captured.
Private John E. Atwell, wounded and captured.
Private William H. Atwell, wounded and captured.
Private George Anderson, captured.
Private John Breon, captured.
Private Theodore S. Burns, wounded and captured.
Private James M. Cooper, captured.
Private Sylvester M. Carr, captured.
Private John N. Davis, captured.
Private Archibald S. Ervin, killed.
Private John W. Fuller, captured.
Private Solomon T. Holsey, captured.
Private Enos Hockett, mortally wounded and captured.
Private John T. Hobbs, captured.
Private William Hamilton, wounded and captured.
Private William H. Hudson, wounded and captured.
Private Daniel King, captured.
Private Francis M. Kitterman, captured.
Private George W. Kitterman, wounded and captured.
Private George Lowe, captured.
Private James M. Lamb, captured.

Private David Lowe, captured.
Private John Marrow, captured.
Private Thomas W. Moffatt, captured.
Private James Moore, captured.
Private James H. McCune, captured.
Private James Morrison, captured.
Private Samuel T. McFall, wounded and captured.
Private Henry McKowan, captured.
Private Horace O. Owen, captured.
Private Jeremiah Padget, killed.
Private William J. Powell, captured.
Private John E. Richards, captured.
Private Francis M. Scott, captured.
Private Ferdinand Southard, captured.
Private Marcus L. Spurlock, mortally wounded and captured.
Private William Stinson, mortally wounded and captured.
Private John P. Thomas, captured.
Private James Wright, captured.
Private Daniel C. Wolfe, wounded and captured.

COMPANY I.

Captain Joseph B. Gedney, captured.
Lieutenant George R. Houston, captured.
Lieutenant Walter S. Johnson, captured.
First Sergeant Henry Jaquiss, captured.
Sergeant Henry Dodge, killed.
Sergeant Oliver H. Perry, captured.
Corporal James C. Hartly, wounded and captured.
Corporal George Athey, captured.
Corporal Truman E. Gilbert, wounded and captured.
Corporal John B. Adamson, captured.
Corporal James L. Stone, captured.
Fifer James N. Hodges, captured.
Wagoner George Holbrook, captured.
Private Jacob A. Bower, captured.
Private John C. Baggs, captured.
Private Josephus Brown, wounded and captured.
Private Andrew I. Braymen, killed.
Private Simeon Baker, captured.
Private James Baker, wounded and captured.
Private Levi Copple, wounded and captured.
Private David Conger, wounded and captured.
Private Henry W. Davis, wounded and captured.
Private James F. Denvon, captured.
Private Reuben Falouer, captured.

APPENDIX.

Private Isaac Frost, captured.
Private Benjamin F. Guy, captured.
Private Cyrus W. Gibson, wounded.
Private George W. Gibson, killed.
Private William M. Harvey, wounded and captured.
Private Dillman Hutchison, wounded and captured.
Private John H. Harris, killed.
Private David John, captured.
Private William Jarvis, captured.
Private Joan Kingsberry, wounded and captured.
Private Rezzel Lewis, captured.
Private John W. Morgan, captured.
Private William F. Marshall, captured.
Private Isaac O. Medis, captured.
Private James M. Odell, captured.
Private Orin Parks, captured.
Private Samuel E. Pugh, mortally wounded.
Private Horace E. Park, wounded and captured.
Private Edward Streepy, captured.
Private Isaac Streepy, captured.
Private Henry W. Stephenson, captured.
Private George Sutton, captured.
Private William H. Thompson, wounded and captured.

COMPANY K.

Captain John Lambert, captured.
Lieutenant John A. Hurlburt, captured.
Sergeant Josiah T. Young, wounded and captured.
Sergeant Eli Moak, captured.
Corporal Benjamin Kimbrell, captured.
Corporal James W. Taylor, captured.
Corporal Edward Eads, captured.
Corporal James Moneyhan, captured.
Corporal Luther C. Bailey, wounded and captured.
Fifer William P. A. Carter, captured.
Private Henry H. Andrew, captured.
Private Allen M. Bailey, captured.
Private Wesley Banister, killed.
Private Levi Banister, captured.
Private George W. Brott, mortally wounded and captured.
Private Thomas Barker, captured.
Private Samuel T. Boales, captured.
Private Aaron A. Campbell, captured.
Private Thomas H. Case, captured.
Private Joseph Chambers, captured.

Private Henry W. Cline, killed.
Private William S. Collins, wounded.
Private Nathan Hummel, killed.
Private Jacob Hager, captured.
Private William G. Jackson, captured.
Private James D. Johnston, captured.
Private William W. Keeling, captured.
Private Elisha Kenworthy, captured.
Private Conrad Kirkendall, wounded and captured.
Private Joseph Morford, captured.
Private Jackson Maxwell, wounded and captured.
Private James A. Murphy, captured.
Private Daniel Oneil, captured.
Private Jacob G. Potts, captured.
Private Jordan Pike, killed.
Private Edwin Robins, captured.
Private Byron Richmond, mortally wounded and captured.
Private Charles B. Reed, captured.
Private William Stephens, captured.
Private Charles B. Smith, captured.
Private Robert Turner, captured.
Private James T. Thair, captured.
Private Reuben M. Tharpe, captured.
Private John Thomas, captured.
Private George Wiggins, captured.
Private Smith V. Walker, killed.
Private Abraham P. Waugh, mortally wounded and captured.
Private William J. Young, captured.

www.ingramcontent.com/pod-product-compliance
Lightning Source LLC
Chambersburg PA
CBHW031943230426
43672CB00010B/2025